CONCILIUM

CONCILIUM 2006/2

THEOLOGY IN A WORLD OF SPECIALIZATION

Edited by
Erik Borgman and Felix Wilfred

SCM Press · London

Published by SCM Press, 9–17 St Albans Place, London N1 0NX

Copyright © Stichting Concilium

English translations copyright © 2006 SCM-Canterbury Press Ltd

All rights reserved. No part of this publication may be
reproduced, stored in a retrieval system, or transmitted,
in any form or by any means, electronic, mechanical, photocopying,
recording or otherwise, without the prior written permission of
Stichting Concilium, Erasmusplein 1,
6525 HT Nijmegen, The Netherlands

ISBN 0 334 03088 9

Printed and bound in Great Britain by
William Clowes Ltd, Beccles, Suffolk

Concilium Published February, April, June, October
December

Contents

Introduction: Theology in a World of Specialization
ERIK BORGMAN AND FELIX WILFRED 7

I. Fragmentation and Specialization: The Social and Academic Situation . . . 11

The Social Background to the Process of Differentiation in Society and the Life Worlds of Human Beings
KARL GABRIEL 13

Theology in the Modern University: Whither Specialization?
FELIX WILFRED 24

II. Fragmentation and Specialization: Issues for Theology . . . 33

Theology and Religious Studies in an Age of Fragmentation
SHEILA GREEVE DAVANEY 35

'Many Have Undertaken . . . and I too Decided': The One Story or the Many?
ELAINE WAINWRIGHT 45

Theological Ethics without Theology: Assessing Theological-Ethical Reflection of Moral Challenges Posed by Pluralism in Relation to Theology
CHRISTOPH BAUMGARTNER 53

Church History without God or without Faith?
WILLEM FRIJHOFF 65

III. Fragmentation and Specialization: Attempts to Reconnect 77

From Shaken Foundations to a Different Integrity: Spirituality as Response to Fragmentation
  MARY GREY 79

Theologies of the South: Incarnate and Holistic
  DIEGO IRARRAZABAL 88

Who Framed Clodovis Boff? Revisiting the Controversy of 'Theologies of the Genitive' in the Twenty-First Century
  MARCELLA ALTHAUS-REID 99

IV. Fragmentation and Specialization: Theology and Interdisciplinarity 109

Theology in Relation to the Natural Sciences
  PALMYRE OOMEN 111

Theology and the Social Sciences
  RICHARD H. ROBERTS 122

Saving Doctrine: Towards a Theology of Health and Medicine
  STEPHAN VAN ERP 131

Theology: Discipline at the Limits
  ERIK BORGMAN 141

Contributors 153

Introduction:
Theology in a World of Specialization

ERIK BORGMAN AND FELIX WILFRED

Ours is a world of fragmentation. Today's human beings are subject to what social theory calls 'functional differentiation': what once was a unified life world has split up into a variety of functional structures which each have their own inherent form of rationality. Forms of behaviour and routines in the economic world are, for instance, considered inadequate in the world of personal relations. As a consequence, approaches traditionally considered to be all-encompassing and holistic are now themselves seen as limited and specialist. Religion has become a specialized form of behaviour among others, with its own limited functions and specific logic. This behaviour can be described, these functions and this logic can be analysed, which makes the study of religion one academic discipline among others.

This issue of *Concilium* on 'Theology in a World of Specialization' starts with a description of this socio-cultural situation, an analysis of its background and an indication of its consequences by *Karl Gabriel*. In a second article, *Felix Wilfred* makes clear what the consequences of this situation for universities are. There is a tendency for them to mirror the fragmented social worlds in their increasing and ongoing specialization. They try to commodify and commercialize their knowledge in order to be able to market it to today's society. In this situation theology's role is, according to Wilfred, to present the wisdom of the religious and theological traditions and work towards integration of the different and often separated fields of knowledge.

This issue focuses on the question of how theology deals with and reacts to this situation of fragmentation. Traditionally the Christian tradition is viewed as embodying an encompassing view on all activities of human beings. Theology is supposed to study the whole of reality and its different aspects *sub ratione Dei*. However, the academic fragmentation and specialization takes its toll on theology as well.

There are several trends working at the same time. On the one hand, fragmentation in society and in the universities is something that influences the theological situation. *Sheila Greeve Davaney* analyses the position of religious studies and theology in today's universities, especially in the United States. Theology should not consider itself the queen of sciences, but neither should it be a rejected former sibling. Theology should be seen and should behave like one intellectual partner among many and a collegial voice among equals. *Elaine Wainwright* shows the proliferation of approaches, methods and hermeneutics in biblical studies, leading to ongoing differentiation and specialization. She argues that this diversity is in itself biblical and a contribution of biblical studies to contemporary theology. *Christoph Baumgartner* discusses the situation of theological ethics. Here, the tendency towards specialization seems to lead to de-theologizing: to concentration on the ethical discussion which, in a secularized society, is mainly secular and philosophical. Baumgartner makes clear, however, that the norms established by philosophical ethics need to be legitimized by the different normative traditions to which the citizens of a society subscribe. Here he sees an important role for theological ethics and a possibility for strengthening its theological identity. *Willem Frijhoff* makes clear that there is an analogical movement within the field of church history. History as the story of God's developing relationship with humans is part of the Jewish, the Christian and the Islamic traditions. As a consequence of developments in (the perspectives on) scientific inquiry, there is a tendency towards interdisciplinary research into religiousness and the religious. This might result in a more fragmented view of the field that traditionally was covered by 'church history', but also in a view that is more nuanced and multi-focused. No discipline has the monopoly on the religious person.

On the other hand, there are attempts to unify the fragmented and ever more fragmenting discipline of theology around certain specific themes or issues. There is spirituality as an integrating theme not only for theology as a discipline, but also for the lives of human beings in the contemporary, fragmented and differentiated world, as *Mary Grey* makes clear. There are liberation and other contextual theologies that unify theology by stressing its obligation to the preferential option for the poor in the actual situations where they are situated. As is shown by *Diego Irarrazaval*, this in fact means that they are developing forms of theology that are at the same time local and universal, concrete and holistic. *Marcella Althaus-Reid* argues that just stressing unity suggests an attempt to re-install hegemony. She presents alternative models for developing connectivity and avoiding atomization, without the necessity for all to be subject to the power of one view of reality.

In the final part of this issue, several attempts are introduced to re-

Introduction 9

connect theology to other disciplines and fields of knowledge. Thus, theology is taking up its responsibility to see the world as unified in its relation to the God who is its creator.

Palmyre Oomen defends the importance of connecting theology to the natural sciences and presents their interface as a possible field of great theological relevance. Dialogue with the natural sciences and philosophical reflections on their discoveries make it necessary and possible to rethink fundamentally the relationship between God and world. *Richard H. Roberts* argues for the exploration of the field where social sciences and theology meet: the religious and theological views of social reality and the social scientific study of religion and the religious. He argues strongly against religion and theology becoming entrenched, and in favour of a theological dialogue with the complex re-composition of the religio-spiritual field that is currently going on and that is investigated by the social sciences. *Stephan van Erp* defends the theological significance of the field of medicine and what is going on in hospitals, nursing homes and hospices. Traditionally, bodily health was an important issue in Christian tradition and there is an important spiritual and religious aspect in the way we in our societies and cultures deal with suffering and illness. What is necessary is not so much an external criticism of medical practices, but a dialogue between theology and contemporary medicine, so as to view and experience it as the space in which traces of the divine can be encountered.

In conclusion, *Erik Borgman* argues that interdisciplinary research can be a way to rediscover theology as a discipline, not by studying religion as a separate social field, but by studying everything *sub ratione Dei*, under the aspect of God. This issue of *Concilium* makes clear that the current fragmentations and differentiations in society and the university constitute not only a major challenge for theology, but also give theology the opportunity to develop a new contemporary relevance.

I. Fragmentation and Specialization: The Social and Academic Situation

The Social Background to the Process of Differentiation in Society and the Life Worlds of Human Beings

KARL GABRIEL

Introduction

Among the most unmistakable characteristics of modern western societies is their functional differentiation. In Europe the segmentation of social spheres and structures can be traced back to the eleventh century AD when the Investiture Controversy between the German Emperor and the Papacy generated two equal but independent institutions within the one territory.[1] Since the end of the uniformity of medieval culture during the Reformation period, structural and cultural differentiation have been going hand in hand in a kind of 'elective affinity'.[2] Meanwhile we have been aware for about a century that the differentiation of life cycles and areas of function is of necessity linked with what we now call individualization. Georg Simmel has spoken of the intersection of social circles as the unique location of each individual in modern societies.[3] Max Weber as well as Georg Simmel have pointed out that the religious factor plays an important part in the development of the differentiation of societies, so that the question about the fate of religion under the conditions of social differentiation is raised from the beginning of sociological research.

In the first part of the following I will trace the origins of functional differentiation and segmentation in western modernity. The focus of the second step is on the contemporary developments and shaping of the structural segmentation of modern societies. In the process of individualization – as I will show in a third step – the ambivalent consequential effects of social segmentation for the life worlds and lifestyles of human beings emerge in a particularly strong way.

The origins of functional differentiation in western modernity

Presently a consensus is emerging that the origins of modernity ought not to be sought in the age of the Reformation or in the Enlightenment but were already present in the High Middle Ages.[4] Already in the High Middle Ages a kind of structural pluralism which is unique in the history of religion was institutionalized under the umbrella of a symbolically represented culture of uniformity. At the origin of modernity the 'papal revolution' of the eleventh century plays an important part. In the Investiture Controversy the papacy successfully claimed the independence of the 'spiritual realm' and thus constituted a 'secular realm' which was separate as a matter of necessity, as at the same time it placed both of them in a hierarchical relationship of sub- and superordination. Out of this developed a unique pluralism of both powers which no longer allowed for the conventional exit into hierocracy or caesaropapism. Alongside this pluralism it was the development of the medieval city and long-distance trade that generated independent centres of action and extended the links of action.

The revolution of the age of the Reformation did not concern the radicalization of the structural pluralism of the Middle Ages; it was initially rather slowed down and paralysed. What was at stake was rather the implementation of a principally anti-traditional lifestyle. It is well known that Weber regarded the overcoming of traditionalism with regard to lifestyle as so unlikely and full of preconditions that for him only religion as the most important power of lifestyle in pre-modern societies could be trusted to achieve this.[5] Weber's starting point was the magic world-view and its interpretation of the world as a 'magic garden' full of spirits, gods and demons acting behind the scenes. From a comparative as well as a historic-genetic point of view Weber sought to reconstruct the particular anti-traditional potential of Jewish-Christian religion. Weber saw their specific characteristic in the fact that in it and only in it tendencies towards the systematization of the world-view are directed towards the elimination of magic from the understanding of the world. A key role for this particular development, according to Weber, belongs to Jewish prophecy as the foundation of a new understanding of God and a new ethic. The ethical God of the covenant corresponds to the prophetic ethic which 'overcomes' the heterogeneous single norms of the magic world-view 'in the interest of a meaningful comprehensive link between lifestyle and the religious goal of salvation'. Weber sees the continuation of this development as originating in the Jewish tradition of prophecy in Christianity, although initially somewhat retarded, as he seeks to show with regard to medieval Catholicism. The softening factors in Catholicism are the weakening of monotheism, the character of the religiousness of the masses as 'relief' (e.g. from the consequences of sin or the fear of death), the neutralizing of the charismatic nature of religion through the differentiation of the monastic virtue spirituality and its reintegration through the treasury of grace into the institution of grace, the Church. The Reformation – Weber asserts – disrupts this construction of balance and compromise. Lutheranism revives some of the elements of the Old Testament image of God and heightens the problem of theodicy and grace through its rejection of the medieval 'economics of grace' and the devaluation of the monastic 'works of supererogation'. At the same time Lutheran Christianity begins to direct the newly released powers towards an understanding of professional vocation which carried within it the promise of religious reward. For Weber it is only in Calvinism and Puritanism that 'that great historical process in religions of the elimination of magic from the world, which originates in ancient Jewish prophecy, and together with Hellenistic scientific thought begins to reject all magic means of seeking salvation through superstition and crime'[6] comes to its end. Calvinism and Puritanism with their doctrine of predestination heighten the problem of theodicy and grace. The absolute chasm between human beings and God, which does not permit any instances of mediation, transforms the magic garden of times past into the religiously meaningless, real-life cosmos of things and events which finds itself under the severe verdict of 'idolatry'. The absolute situation being other than God as well as other than the world, in which human beings find themselves, only allows for a rational relationship towards the latter: this takes the form of domination of the world through ascetic professional labour as God's instruments and for his glory. This heightens theocentrism to the point that on the level of practical lifestyle it is as it were derailed: the success with regard to methodical-rational lifestyle in profession and economy becomes the reason to know salvation, even if this 'reason' is not really rational.

To summarize: in medieval Catholicism, in Lutheranism and finally in the sectarian piety of the Puritans Weber saw the realization of stages of a denial of the world, which emptied life of its natural assimilation to the past, of its reliance on the regular structures of magic and finally of the periodical relief through confession, until finally the Puritans rendered the world a realm which was as a matter or principle devoid of magic and where perseverance would become a lifelong struggle. Without the Jewish-Christian tradition – according to Weber – and with him in the present, for example,

Wolfgang Schluchter and Franz-Xaver Kaufmann – the anti-traditionalism within modern western culture would be unthinkable. Only here does a world-view emerge that forces us to constant action/intervention/change in the world and challenges us to rational domination of the world. Ultimately this world-view was to be carried by the bourgeoisie with its lifestyle which was oriented towards moderation and the steady accumulation of wealth.

Even with its darkest sides Christianity is intertwined with the process of the functional differentiation of western societies. After the demise of Church unity in the Reformation the new Christian denominations proved themselves to be principally 'incapable of peace' during the century of the wars of religion.[7] For the sake of mere survival this forced the emancipation of the emerging sphere of state domination from the control of religion and the Church. For religion in its denominational form this means being under the control of the state and the beginning of its public neutralization. The development of a general universal concept of religion as distinct from the historic understanding of religion of the denominationally divided Christianity was one of the reactions to this situation and for some time the churches were able to avert the fundamental neutralization and privatization of religion.

Today, with regard to the origins of the structural differentiation and cultural pluralization of modernity, it is, apart from the High Middle Ages, the seventeenth century which is of particular interest. In addition to the structures of society and the state it is also the sphere of the cultural integration of society which begins to separate from Christianity in its ecclesial-denominational form. The point of reference is now the common nature of humanity which is above denominational strife; its protection in the form of natural law and human rights is the obligation of the state.

The basic pattern of the functional differentiation in modern societies

During the late eighteenth and nineteenth centuries the general dethronement and limitation of tradition was coupled with the emergence of a new pluralism of structures and functions, ranging from the economic, the political and the religious to family structures. They all developed their own foundations of meaning, increased the extent of social complexity and rendered the 'whole' more and more impenetrable.[8]

Through the bourgeoisie and the revolutions experienced by it – the cultural and political as well as industrial – a kind of society came to the

The Social Background to the Process of Differentiation

fore in the West which has right up to the present day shaped and formed the living conditions and the lifestyle of human beings in a way that is unique in history.[9] This kind of society emerged against the background of the tradition of medieval Christianity. Its origins are clearly visible since the High Middle Ages with the double representation of the one Christendom in Pope and Emperor and the emerging urban bourgeoisie developing along the long-distance trading routes. This kind of society can be sketched in broad terms as having the following structural and cultural characteristics.

Out of the feudal ordering of the state there gradually emerges, through the political revolution of the bourgeoisie, the *civil state under the rule of law*. Here the bourgeoisie takes over the structural entity of the modern centralized state developed through the concentration and monopolization of power in the hands of the princes. It loosens the ties of feudal restriction and gives it the shape of a nation state. Challenged by the movements of social reform during the nineteenth century and moved forward by its internal contradictions, the western type of the state develops via different routes during the twentieth century into the modern democratic (social) state. As a result we find nowadays an independent sphere of the political, which is legitimized by the rule of law, and the social ordering of the state with a high level of idiosyncratic complexity.

The revolutions of the bourgeoisie set free a sphere of 'civil society' which is separate from the state, and which is one of the central characteristics of bourgeois modernity. It is first and foremost the realm of the free exchange of goods between autonomous economic subjects, the sphere of the capitalist nationalization of the market. Bourgeois society constitutes itself primarily as an economic workforce which presumes that everyone is available for deployment in the interests of this kind of society. Its central form of integration is the mechanism of the market: starting from the labour market, through goods markets to market-like structures in the cultural sphere. In the interplay of natural science and technology the mechanism of the market triggered an unprecedented release of all productive powers. This enabled a rise in the standard of living even of those who had nothing to sell other than their labour. The state protection of social security against the risks inherent in the life of wage labourers played a decisive role in the gradual change of the living condition of the proletariat. Among the resulting problems of material success following the nationalization of the market were the *degeneration of cultural forms of social integration over against material forms of system integration*.

Alongside modern structures in politics, the economy and society there develops the social form of the *modern family*. Prepared for by the increase in value of the private domestic realm in Protestantism, the structures of the individual family separated themselves out from the family structures of the 'entire household' of the master, in which without distinction and as a matter of course all relatives and servants living in the household had belonged. Through the breakdown of the corporate ties of social life, romantic love became the motive and the reason for marriage. On this basis family life developed in the bourgeois society of the nineteenth century as a separate sphere of private intimacy, a realm of emotional mutual recognition. At the heart of the new family life and sense of the family was an emotional bond between mother and child, which replaced the earlier distance that originated not least from a high level of infant mortality. This implies a new polarized cultural stylization of gender roles. The newly emerging sphere of familial domesticity was regarded as the proper realm of the woman. It was by nature her vocation and destiny. As the family oriented towards emotion and mutual recognition formed the woman's realm, so the sphere of mutual exchange, of labour, of professional and public matters became the realm of the man. In order to 'stand his ground' in this sphere man by nature is endowed with a set of gifts different from those of a woman. Originating from the bourgeoisie, the model of the family advances victoriously into all social classes. It changes in this process of universalization, but nevertheless determines the lifestyle and the normal biography of human beings up to the transitions of the present day.[10]

Part and parcel of the transformation of society is also the *new social form of Christendom*. The separation of the spiritual from the secular opening up during the High Middle Ages now receives the form of an independent sphere of life for the ecclesial-religious, distinct from all other areas of life. The feudal lifestyle, legitimized by religion and kept in shape through 'church discipline' which set the norms for all areas of life, is broken up. The differentiation of the life of society gets under way – empowered through the origin of modern bourgeois society in the social pattern of medieval Christianity – as emancipation from institutional Christianity. The process of transformation becomes at once a process of religious institutionalization and secularization. On the one hand the contents of meaning of the Christian tradition are socially rooted in the realm of the Church which is separate from all other areas of life. This begins with the social separation of the civil community from the church community. It proceeds with the separation of the socialization and lifestyle of the clergy from those of the rest of society

The Social Background to the Process of Differentiation

and finds its expression in the reinforcement of an ecclesial dogmatic Christianity on the level of church teaching and church theology. In Catholicism already during the nineteenth century, in Protestantism only in the twentieth century, an independent ecclesial institutional social form of Christianity emerges which in turn fights more or less successfully for its emancipation from the claims of omnipotence on the part of the modern state.

Alongside the institutionalization of Christianity there is a concurrent secularization of spheres of the life of society, of social zones and regions and of social classes and milieux of life. The Church's influence on politics, the economy and family life is reduced. Urbanization goes alongside a high level of secularization, and the newly emerging economic and educated bourgeoisie on the one hand, and large parts of the proletariat on the other, distance themselves from the institutionalized forms of Christianity. At the same time traditionally minded groups of the population and social movements which seek to resist the transformation of society seek the closeness and the protection of church structures. Those groups of the population which have withdrawn from the process of institutionalization neither become un-religious nor can they be described as merely post-Christian. In bourgeoisie a new social form of religion develops which neither completely rejects the Christian tradition nor does it sever all ties with the institution of the Christian Church. Their characteristic is the transformation of religion into piety. It reflects the immediate accessibility of the religious for the individual and alongside it the subjectivization of the objective religious contents of the Christian tradition. Into the background of the bourgeois culture of reflection that had partly been shaped by Christianity itself it absorbs the new experiences of the bourgeoisie and it gives them their syncretistic character. Even in the case of religion we can observe a strong generalization of the new social form of religion on the part of the bourgeoisie. With the emergence of bourgeois society religion becomes a private matter in so far as the form of participation in the religious ecclesial sphere becomes a matter of the private decision of the individual. Religious freedom is understood as securing free access to religion as well as the freedom to make decisions over against the totalitarian claims of religion.[11]

Today the full consequences of modernity show themselves in a heightening of functional differentiation with the development and growing independence of functional part-systems of society.[12] The increasing distinctiveness comes from the intensity of their specialization, their autonomy and their self-legitimization as well as their enlargement into global dimensions. Thus the economic activity which is based on the monetary economy and markets has freed itself from being concerned with foreign travel as well as having taken on the global dimension of a capitalist global economy. Similar things can be said about the part-system of state politics which has, on the one hand, developed its own internal logic in the context of the nation state, and at the same time seems to be increasingly drawn into confederations of states and even into a global system of nation states. Science as a further leading functional system of modern societies on the one hand has shifted internally from the search for certainty to unlimited methodological questioning; on the other hand it has taken on more and more the form of the contexts of communication of the global society. As a consequence of heightened functional differentiation the life of society as a whole is becoming altogether more pluralist and more diverse, and increasingly places itself outside central hierarchical control. The increasing loss of hierarchical control undermines the typical claim of the Enlightenment and classical science to be able to control ultimately all aspects of life centrally through the spreading of enlightenment and knowledge.[13]

In this situation *religion* finds itself in the peculiar role of being at once a postulate and a desiderate. It is needed absolutely everywhere. On the basis of a variety of justifications it is deemed to be more necessary than ever. Here we begin to see a break with the way religion is presented as the central theme in the context of modernity. On the one hand there is a contrast to the marginalization of the structures of actual religious systems. From the perspective of the leading systems of the economy, politics and science, actual religious systems are a largely negligible entity. Its interpretations and moral postulates also increasingly bounce off the surface of the enclosed space of relationships and family life. In addition, the theologically driven thematic purification and internal processes of rationalization of the structures of religious systems tend to heighten the marginalization further and to ossify it rather than to break it up. Thus a chasm is developing between religion as a postulate on the one hand and actual institutionalized religion on the other.

Problems arising from functional differentiation: individualization of life context and lifestyle

As an example for the analytical clarification of the problems arising from functional differentiation we may look at the theoretical construction of individualization.[14] The continuing and heightening modernization in the already modernized societies of the West lets modern society appear as an individualized society. The complex term 'individualization' is initially used to discuss phenomena which point to a changed relationship between human beings and their hitherto largely prescribed forms of life. More and more people find themselves freed from those prerogatives previously regarded as given, such as family life, gender roles, lifelong employment to earn a living, as well as regional and religious ties. As statistics show, conventional life forms do not disappear altogether – actually the majority of the population continues to move within them – but they have lost the character of being given and taken for granted. In the light of the availability of alternatives they become objects of complicated processes of choice and decisions. Thus the character of the social location of the individual is changed. Individuals become socially dislocated in so far as social locations which may have been taken for granted in the past are less and less available to them. Their location happens generally by their own choice – at least in the light of available alternatives society treats and describes it as the free choice of individuals.

Linked with the *emancipation from obsolete ties of tradition* and the pluralization of life forms is also a *de-traditionalization of the interpretations of the meaning of life*. Obsolete interpretations lose their meaning as given and as destiny in the light of emerging alternatives. Even in the search for the meaning of life individuals themselves are required to choose among a number of available possible alternatives. This is a lifelong task.

Emancipation is thus not to be equated with a clear and unlimited gain of freedom. Rather, the social obligations are heightened too. Not only the life forms and interpretations of life are being individualized but also social obligations. Individuals who have been freed from obsolete life forms and interpretations face the fact that some social prerogatives, which now concern them as individuals, are not available to them. The prerogatives arise first of all from the anonymous power of an increasingly narrow labour market. Traditional norms with regard to the average life story and everyday life through social background, sex or age are replaced by new norms according to the phases of an 'average working life' and the time schemes of a 'regular working day'.[15] The power of the labour market as part of life becomes part of the life of the individual at earlier and earlier stages and forces them to develop an individual and competitive perspective on life. It is not very different with regard to the power of public provision for care. The assurance of the collective destiny of risky wage labour has developed into a complex system of regulations of the rights of individuals to which individuals are required to conform if they want to avoid being at a serious disadvantage.

As a process of emancipation from given life forms and social ties alongside increasing anonymous relationships of dependency which concern human beings as individuals, individualization does not mean an increase of freedom and autonomy as such. At the heart of an individualized praxis of life there is instead the obligation to develop one's own life story and to be given responsibility for one's own destiny. Reference and referral to one's self therefore become a constant with regard to lifestyle. This, however, does not render impossible the existence and the creation of ties of solidarity, although it creates a new set of conditions under which they develop. Social ties are selected as part of each individual's life plans and have to be tried and tested in a process of negotiation. As selective ties they have themselves more preconditions and are more precarious, while on the other hand they have an inherent self-binding strength.

With regard to the level of individual lifestyle, this means that the integration of the individual into society is tied to participation in and competence in the handling of the multitude of different directions and interpretations of life. Individuals have available to them a variety of interpretations of an (ordered) world and of a (good) life offered to them in religious traditions and secular interpretations of the world. These relate to both the horizontal (transcending different spheres of life) and the vertical (encompassing one's life story as a whole) integration of meaning of one's own life. Authentic solutions of the problem of meaning are placed more and more into the hands of the individual and require their own effort of interpretation. In modern society tensions between individual religiousness and religion as a system of belief are therefore inevitable. What is nowadays being articulated as the concept of postmodernity refers to a radicalization of pluralism on the structural and individual levels and is by no means an actual break with modernity.

Translated by Natalie K. Watson

Notes

1. Franz-Xaver Kaufmann, 2000, *Wie überlebt das Christentum?*, Freiburg im Breisgau: Herder, p. 76.
2. This formulation is based on Max Weber, 1972, 'Die protestantische Ethik und der Geist des Kapitalismus', in *Gesammelte Aufsätze zur Religionssoziologie* I, Tübingen: Mohr, p. 83.

The Social Background to the Process of Differentiation 23

3. Georg Simmel, 1968 (first published in 1908), *Soziologie. Untersuchungen über die Formen der Vergesellschaftung*, Berlin, pp. 305ff.
4. Wolfgang Schluchter, 1988, *Religion und Lebensführung*, vol. 2, Frankfurt am Main: Suhrkamp, pp. 437ff.
5. Schluchter, *Religion*, pp. 382ff.
6. Weber, 'Die protestantische Ethik', pp. 94f., note 2.
7. Wolfhard Pannenberg, 1988, *Christentum in einer säkularisierten Welt*, Freiburg im Breisgau: Herder.
8. Cf. Niklas Luhmann, 1997, *Die Gesellschaft der Gesellschaft*, 2 vols, Frankfurt am Main: Suhrkamp.
9. Cf. Karl Gabriel, 2000, *Christentum zwischen Gesellschaft und Postmoderne*, 7th edn, Freiburg im Breisgau: Herder, pp. 69ff.
10. Franz-Xaver Kaufmann, 1995, *Die Zukunft der Familie im vereinten Deutschland. Gesellschaftliche und politische Bedingungen*, Munich: Beck, pp. 19ff.
11. Kaufmann, *Wie überlebt das Christentum?*, pp. 78ff.
12. Cf. Karl Gabriel, 1996, 'Gesellschaft im Umbruch – Wandel des Religösen', in Hans-Joachim Höhn (ed.), *Krise der Immanenz. Religion an der Grenze der Moderne*, Frankfurt am Main: Fischer.
13. Franz-Xaver Kaufmann, 1995, 'Zur Einführung: Probleme und Wege einer historischen Einschätzung des II. Vatikanischen Konzils', in Franz-Xaver Kaufmann and Arnold Zingerle (eds), 1995, *Vatikanum II und Modernisierung. Historische, theologische und sociologische Perspektiven*, Paderborn: Schöningh, pp. 18–24.
14. Ulrich Beck and Elisabeth Beck-Gernsheim, 1994, 'Individualisierung in modernen Gesellschaften – Perspectiven und Kontroversen einer subjektorientierten Soziologie', in Ulrich Beck and Elisabeth Beck-Gernsheim (eds), 1994, *Riskante Freiheiten*, Frankfurt am Main: Suhrkamp, pp. 10–39.
15. Martin Kohli, 1988, 'Normalbiographie und Individualität: Zur institutionellen Dynamik des gegenwärtigen Lebenslaufregimes', in Hans-Georg Brose and Bernhard Hildebrand (eds), 1988, *Vom Ende des Individuums zur Individualität ohne Ende*, Opladen: Leske & Budrich, pp. 33–54.

Theology in the Modern University: Whither Specialization?

FELIX WILFRED

The functional differentiation that distinguishes modern society from its predecessors logically leads to specialization and the creation of professionals, making society and its subsystems increasingly complex in the process. As an integral part of the modern society, religion too undergoes the same kind of developments, which in effect means a departure from the more comprehensive role it played in earlier times. Universities obviously reflect these transformations in the nature of society.

In recent years, the conventional ideals and goals of the university, developed in times other than our own, have been undergoing profound changes. These also lead us to reflect on the place and role of theology as a discipline in the new contexts of education and research. To enter into a debate on whether theology is a science on a par with other sciences in a university is to beat a dead horse. The question today has shifted to new terrains, and we are facing new challenges. The justification, if any, for the place of theology in a university lies somewhere other than in its credentials as a 'science' (*Wissenschaft*). Added to this is the fact that in many western universities, theology has turned out to be an orphan discipline unsupported by the public, with decreasing funds and with ever fewer students.

Moreover, contemporary theology has to contend with a situation in which institutions of higher education, such as universities, no longer have the classical *pursuit of truth* as their goal, or the knowledge of the laws of nature, but are increasingly oriented towards being evaluated in terms of pragmatic objectives of output and capacity to meet particular targets. Disciplines are evaluated by the no-nonsense criteria of viability, which in effect means marketability, and the whole system tends to create individuals capable of acquiring power and wealth. In fact, we observe a growing connection between the academic pursuit through specialization and the world of industry and commerce which stand to benefit from such a pursuit.

If this is the situation today, under what conditions would theology be able to reinvent its place in the modern university that has become a symbol of specialization, and on that score a platform for business and commercial interests? Will theology be able to respond to the needs of today's world of knowledge and human predicament, and therefore legitimately find a place in the university and in institutions of higher education? This will be the ultimate objective of our enquiry and reflection in this article. I shall draw also from my own experience of teaching in a state university in India for the past few years.

Three temptations of theology

The first temptation of theology is *self-isolation*. It is the refusal to step out from the narrow confines of a dated model of theology whose primary role, in the description of Avery Dulles, 'is to reflect on the teaching of the Church, elucidate what has been taught and to propose what could be officially taught in the future'.[1] If such is the understanding of theology, then it may not find a legitimate place in the public universities. For its scope is too narrow and orientation too sectarian, and it is not clear what public interest it serves in order to claim to be in a state university and stake claims for state funds.

The second temptation is *to believe that theology advances by specialization*, that is, by the process of atomizing theological knowledge into ever-smaller units. The transmutation of theological studies involving confessional commitment into presumed 'neutral' religious studies is a development we are witnessing in some western countries. This change has facilitated the process of specialization in a way and along the lines traditional theology was not used to. The breakup of the field of religious studies in imitation of other disciplines has, no doubt, produced an incredible amount of knowledge. However, if they are to remain more than merely providers of more knowledge and information, theology and religious studies need to ask themselves to what transformations they lead. If this can be expected of all other disciplines, there is reason to expect it all the more from theology and the study of religion.

The classical model of knowledge as quest for truth is replaced today by knowledge as object of production to be organized like other domains in society. The information society tends to think that the quantitative profusion of information amounts to quality and value, and that the *production of more data is equal to greater truth* – a delusion to which theology and religious studies are in danger of falling prey. Theology and religious studies could be easily drawn into the system of modern organization of intellectual work and sciences centred on reputation and marketability.[2] Further, the importance of accumulating specialized information in any discipline, especially in the arts and humanities, as a precondition for progress rests on the premise that they provide the basis for rational choices – something that reflects a particular and historically conditioned conception of development and progress. Theology within the university is tempted to accommodate itself to these presuppositions and mould itself accordingly. Catherine Keller presents a grim picture of the situation in the West as to where addiction to specialization could lead theology:

> The shocking difficulty of creating community even within a departmental faculty reflects more than the problem of narcissistic personalities. The narcissism is itself a symptom of a cultural system, uncritically reproduced in the university, in which performance and production are valued over creativity and community. Most writing is quite explicitly motivated by the demands of the academic marketplace, structured by the economic incentives of tenure and promotion. It is accordingly insipid, stifling any inclinations to poetry or to prophecy.[3]

Exceptionalism is the third temptation of theology. In the modern world an enlightened approach to the study of any reality calls for freedom of enquiry without interference from outside forces. Theology may presume that this does not apply to itself. Any right-thinking person will immediately note the contradiction between the claim to be part of the university system as a discipline, and at the same time the refusal to be subject to academic freedom. The freedom of research and enquiry could be curtailed by intervention through religious authorities or by authoritarian state-machinery.[4] When the curbing of freedom of enquiry in theological studies is built into the structures themselves, as is the case with *covenants and concordats* entered into between religious authorities and the state, it cannot but be viewed as a serious anomaly. Such structural curtailment of freedom in some universities in the West deprives the students and the public of the benefit of highly competent and outstanding teaching faculties, and could be an expression of obscurantist authoritarianism, not consonant with an academic institution which should be guided by rational choices in its organization as well as in the choice of the teaching faculty.

In the past, theology claimed many exceptions, but in the course of time it had to abandon them. The external circumstances and the force of necessity led to the realization that theology could exist without claiming exemptions. A noteworthy instance is the case of theological hermeneutics. It was the merit of Friedrich Schleiermacher to have made us realize that theology does not become any less by subjecting itself, the Bible and even faith to the general laws of hermeneutics without seeking a privileged place.[5] In the long run, this approach helps theology more than one could suspect.

Three assumptions behind specialization

Modern sciences progress through increasing classification, taxonomy, cataloguing etc. Atomization or fragmentation of knowledge through such procedures means affirmation of autonomy in increasing new fields of study as separate and independent ones. This calls for the role of experts and professionals to produce specialized knowledge and manage it. Moreover, this requires also the creation of new institutions and structures oriented to the above purpose.

The fragmentation assisted by these methods is obviously the strength of science. But the dilemma for theology is whether it should shy away from what is considered to be the strength of science – all the more if it wants to claim the character of science and find a niche in the university setting. Or, should it present a different dimension – the dimension of *wholeness and totality*? If the latter is the case, in what way could it be considered a science to be ranked within the *universitas studiorum*? Let us examine some of the assumptions behind specialization in order to see what extent it could be applicable to theological studies.

The first assumption is that the more specialization the more *certain* we are about the truth of a particular reality. On the contrary, what experience shows instead is that uncertainty increases with specialization. The second assumption is that the greater the specialization the *more effective the solutions*. Here again experience seems to tell us that for every one problem solved by specialization there are more that are generated and that defy solution. The third assumption is that the specialization creates *trust* in the experts. Surprisingly, the situation today is such that there is growing erosion of trust in the professionals and experts. For example, beef could be declared 'safe' by experts as happened in the context of bovine spongiform encephalopathy (so-called 'mad cow disease') in the United Kingdom, but then people began to question the ulterior motives of the market behind experts' statements. As Barry Smart notes:

There are no guarantees for trust, merely differing degrees of awareness of and concern over the risks that lie in wait, which in turn expert systems attempt to address, the strategy generally being to seek to minimize or reduce, and where possible remove risks, but also at times to conceal them.[6]

I do not mean to say that specialization is not worth pursuing. Nor am I opposing the modern scientific method for which specialization is very important. I am also not dissuading theology from having its own fields of specialization. What I am trying to say is that there is *no direct correlation between specialization and human growth*. If such is the case, to what extent could theology of the future depend upon specialization?

Let me make some detailed comments on the three assumptions. To think that progress consists in specialization – as many imagine – is to ignore the fact that specialization does not promise to solve all the problems. Rather, what we are experiencing is that specialization which solves one problem, becomes the source of other problems. Moreover, professionalism implies exclusion of others as 'unqualified', implying that these people have nothing to do with human destiny.

One of the distinguishing marks of our time is uncertainty, as many analysts have tried to tell us. In fact, more information has not led us to lessen this uncertainty, rather it has heightened it to an unprecedented level, which raises the question about the ability of science-based knowledge and information to solve human issues and questions. These require more than information. Theology needs to follow a path that leads to finding the *roots of this uncertainty* and address at that level the sciences, and its own claim of being a science, in a completely different social, cultural and knowledge configuration than the space offered by the stereotypical contrast of faith and reason.

Reinventing theology in modern universities: some trajectories

I think it was Karl Barth who said that a good theology does not require advocacy; it proves itself. Theology need not today prove itself to be scientific for its credibility. What it must do is to demonstrate that it serves public interest. The inextricable relationship between fact and value, and the de-construction of a presumed neutrality of the sciences, have rendered it unnecessary for theology today to prove its credentials by its 'scientific' character. The real task in justifying its presence in the university is to show that it serves public interest.

It should be clear then why the reason–faith debate cannot be the premise for theology in the university today. In other words, theology does not find a place in the university because it has something to say that reason is not able to offer. The main assumption that could justify theology in the university is that religious resources have something to contribute to the welfare of humankind and its well-being. The second assumption is that a significant part of humankind, including those in academic life, derive orientations and insights directly or indirectly from religious resources. Now religious sources and beliefs are to be subjected to critical study, so that they could readily serve humanity. As part of the university academic system, religion and theology will be studied critically, but at the same time with an orientation towards the transformation of the self and of society. These are not opposed to each other, but rather they enrich mutually.

It is in this connection that we need to reflect critically on the present scenario of fragmentation in the various disciplines motivated by the need to generate knowledge applicable to the fulfilment of ever more specific and specialized needs. The point at stake is to what extent theology in the university needs to follow this trajectory of modern science. The answer to the question will depend upon the kind of need theology is today expected to respond to. If we take this as the point of departure, then it appears to me that the role of theology has to go in *a different direction*. The purpose of study and enquiry is not only to derive benefits from the atomization of knowledge and its application. There is also an important need for *wholeness* to be attained by relating and interconnecting the various elements and parts, and this process has close affinity with wisdom. 'The whole' here is not understood as an abstract universal that often turns out to be the source of a superiority complex. The whole is rather like a horizon that will accompany the meticulous and detailed pursuit of knowledge in any given sphere. This should be the case all the more for theology, which in the best of Christian tradition has been viewed as wisdom. Wisdom can by no means be an intruder into the university, though, unfortunately, this is the impression we get from many academics, including theologians. The university should be of such an environment that wisdom could be truly at home.

This way of approaching the question pre-empts the dilemma theology and religion are faced with, namely, how could something that addresses the whole have place and meaning in a world that is characterized by growing specialization?[7] In the past, it was the whole that was thought to be of a higher order, representing fullness and perfection compared to the part, or fragment, which was supposed to be imperfect. Ironically, today, it is religion, which deals with the whole in a world that has specialization as its focus, that is compelled to defend itself.

Why is the sense of whole important in the university at all? Why should theology follow the direction of the whole? There are areas in human life that are so crucial as to become a matter of general concern, requiring broader ethical and humanistic perspectives that may not concern the professionals and specialists. Such, for example, is the case of economics. If one were to argue, for instance, that only professionals in the field could pronounce on economics, it could result in the colossal neglect of issues of economic justice and equity. Holistic considerations and broader perspectives rather than exclusive reliance on the experts and their opinions are to be given their due place in the study of economics.

Expertise and specialization obliterate a large portion of reality with which people are familiar in everyday life. Further, to make people inhabit a world created by the professional mandarins is to ignore the resources of the people, their agency and their experience, in the pursuit of truth, which has a holistic dimension. The danger for theology is that it can join hands with the world of experts and professionals, and in the process can get isolated and ensconced in theological laboratories. Ironically, one could even become proud of this isolation! Hence we could say that while theology has to conform to the canons of science with its procedures, logic and method, it cannot share the view that science has little to do with society. This responsibility cannot be abdicated because of reputation or excellence in the particular discipline, cultivated by means of isolation.

Another way of expressing the point is to say that theology in the university shall not blindly follow the other sciences in specialization, but should rather focus more directly on issues raised by other systems in society but not solved by them. This is a way to cater to the aspiration for the whole. Here we need to be aware of the overall situation of late modern society in which we realize that instrumental reason, which is very much at work in the dynamics of specialization and application, has not been able to respond to some of the pressing human issues – poverty, violence, inequality, problems of bioethics, genetic manipulation, etc. It would not be exact to describe the situation simply as that of absence of *meaning*, in order to find a foothold for theology. However, we need to go further than that.

Whereas knowledge is divisible and can be atomized, the *reality* with which theology deals is indivisible. Hence atomization or specialization in theology has only a limited validity and legitimacy, and it cannot imitate the empirical sciences. This needs to be stated against the view of Heidegger,[8] who argues that theology is closer to the natural sciences than to philosophy, which would imply that the path of specialization would also be that of theology. In fact the development of theology and its growing dissolution into religious studies is nothing but an unwitting realization of Heidegger's argument.

Obviously, there is a rightful place for specialization within theology. But the more specific role of theology in the university would be one of *integration*, namely that of relating the various spheres of life and providing a sense of the whole, which is the indispensable horizon for the emergence of meaning and value. It is like a family whose wholeness cannot be replaced by the various segmental issues it deals with – finance, health-care, education of children, etc.

Finally, we must also admit that the role of theology in the university has become more difficult and challenging when we consider the change the *concept of the university* itself has undergone. The contemporary university is placed in the context of the information society. Whereas in the past the goal of *formation* was at the origins of many universities and the pursuit of human values defined their concrete mode of working (we could think of John Henry Newman's *Idea of a University*, for example), today the production and dissemination of information seem to define the universities and their excellence. This makes the place and role of theology in the contemporary university even more challenging and difficult than in the times when formation was the focus of attention.

Conclusion

Today, the argument for theology in the university is to be based not on the claim that it is a science that can be studied like other sciences, but on the fact that it represents an important source of wisdom, the interpretation and study of which could contribute to transforming the plight of humanity and the world. Can wisdom be a stranger in the university?

The question of the extent of specialization needs to be gauged by this yardstick. This imposes a restructuring of theology and reinvention of it in such a way that it is directed to larger goals. One such goal would be inter-religious understanding and harmony, whose importance is so evident when we witness the situation of escalating religious conflicts in the world. In this regard, there is also the need to develop *comparative theology* in the university.[9] Moreover, theology needs to develop *a sense of wholeness* which could contribute to solving some of the pressing questions affecting humanity. It is towards such ideals that the study of theology is directed in the state universities in the developing world like India and China through departments of Christian Studies.

There is obviously a role for theology in relation to the Christian community, which could be fulfilled by studying theology in the context of private institutions like seminaries. It is not understandable that theology should find a place in a state university if the Christian community is the primary end. The growing realization today, that science needs to shift its concerns from matters of fact to considerations of value, can only facilitate the role theology is called upon to play in our society and the present world.

Notes

1. Avery Dulles, 2002, 'Le statut de la théologie dan les université catholique aux États-Unis', in François Bousquet, Henri-Jérôme Gagey et al. (eds), *La responsabilité des théologiens. Mélanges offerts à Joseph Doré*, Paris: Desclée, p. 295.
2. Cf. Richard Whitely, 2000, *Intellectual and Social Organization of the Sciences*, 2nd edn, Oxford: Oxford University Press.
3. Catherine Keller, 1991, 'Toward an Emancipatory Wisdom', in David Ray Griffin and Joseph C. Hough, Jr (eds), *Theology and the University*, New York: State University of New York Press, p. 133.
4. The intervention of religious authorities is well known and does not require any comment. As for state authorities, we are not sure to what extent the study of theology and Christianity in China, for example, is free from state interventions.
5. Cf. Werner Jeanrond, 1991, *Theological Hermeneutics: Development and Significance*, New York: Crossroad.
6. Barry Smart, 1999, *Facing Modernity: Ambivalence, Reflexivity and Modernity*, Delhi: Sage Publications, p. 8.
7. Cf. Peter Beyer, 2000, *Religion and Globalisation*, London: Sage Publications; New Delhi: Thousand Oaks.
8. Cf. Martin Heidegger, 2002, 'Phenomenology and Theology', in John D. Caputo (ed.), *The Religious*, Oxford: Blackwell, pp. 49–56.
9. We are far away from the times when Protestants and Catholics had to prove the claims of their respective confessions by setting up separate departments of theology, though the past legacy seems still to linger on in some parts of the world.

II. Fragmentation and Specialization: Issues for Theology

Theology and Religious Studies in an Age of Fragmentation[1]

SHEILA GREEVE DAVANEY

The rising crisis

Theology's definition and role in the intellectual life of the West have significantly changed over the millennia. During the emergent centuries of Christianity reflection on God and discourse about God primarily served the dual purposes of enhancing the spiritual lives of Christians and shaping the newly formed institutions of the Church as Christianity sought to define its identity and borders. By the medieval period, and especially with the rise of the great universities of the Middle Ages, theology continued to be pursued as a spiritual practice to nurture believers' relationship with the divine, but it also developed more and more into a discipline predicated on rational reflection and knowledge attained from the world. In both these modes theology reigned at the apex of western thought as the unifying centre of Christian reflection and practice and as the primary site for adjudicating disputes not only about how best to know and serve God but concerning what would count as truth about the world as well.

Theology's role as 'queen of the sciences', as articulator of a holistic interpretation of reality within which all finite entities found their proper place and in relation to which all intellectual activity was organized and regulated, was greatly challenged by the advent of modernity. By the Renaissance, Christianity's hold on European life was already in transition as admiration for ancient Greek culture grew, new forms of humanism emerged and the political and economic structures of medieval European life shifted away from feudalism. The Protestant Reformation and the century of religious wars that followed contributed greatly to the undermining of the old order as the Holy Roman Empire dissolved and the modern nation state was born. And in that new order both religion and theology would come to occupy new and very different locations in Europe and eventually in the United States. It is important to understand how such shifts took place for they continue to reverberate in our contemporary social, political and academic worlds. In many accounts, the Protestant Reformation plays a pivotal role in the emergence of modernity.

In the aftermath of the Reformation, religious renewal and new forms of theological reflection found expression as Protestantism took myriad shapes and Roman Catholicism underwent internal change in the Counter-Reformation. But the outcome of these changes was not only new religious vitalities but also religious wars and political strife. Religious conflict, between Catholics and Protestants and between various Protestant groups, devastated much of Europe. As Catholic hegemony declined, the new religious pluralism did not result in a world of peaceful coexistence but one in which bloodshed, economic chaos and political turmoil were the common realities. In an environment in which religious, political and economic realities all were intimately intertwined, the crises of the sixteenth and seventeenth centuries affected every area of European life. It was out of and in response to these myriad crises that the modern European world was born.

By the seventeenth century Europeans faced the profound problem of how to adjudicate differences, including religious differences, when one dominant authority no longer held sway and in its stead a multiplicity of perspectives vied for control and power. Instead of at least the illusion of a unified religious, political and economic world, the modern context was increasingly characterized by plurality, fragmentation and competing authorities. Moreover, expanded exploration and the spread of colonialism to the far reaches of the globe brought information about cultures and religions very different from the prevalent Christianity and minority Judaism of Europe. Such information would, with ever greater intensity, challenge the assumptions of Christian and western theistic superiority as the modern period unfolded. Accompanying all of these shifts was the emergence of a new contender for intellectual dominance, modern science; as the hegemony of religion was progressively undermined, reason, especially in its scientific modes, offered interpretations of reality that challenged the religious pictures that had shaped the imagination of the West for millennia, and further developed new criteria for ascertaining what would count as truth in an ever more pluralistic world. As once religion, and theology as its formal expression, had regulated beliefs and practices, now reason, especially science, became the touchstone of modern life especially in what came to be known as the Enlightenment.

Theology and religion in the modern world

The responses to these crises and new developments in relation to religion were varied. Different nation states understood the role of religion in society in distinct ways. A growing hostility toward religion in France culminated in the anti-religious rhetoric and actions of the Revolution, while in the German-speaking lands there continued the affirmation of a positive relation between religion and national identity in the German Enlightenment and in developments such as Pietism. Various other religious options took shape within and outside of Christianity. A rational religion, unencumbered by outmoded dogmas or ecclesial authority, was articulated by Deists; and Jews, convinced of the importance of adapting Judaism to the modern context, formulated a new and modern Reformed Judaism in the nineteenth century. In many instances, a new spirit of religious tolerance and the affirmation of the freedom to practise religion received clearer articulation in laws and in the constitutions of new nations such as the United States.

Accompanying these new realities was what has in some ways become one of the central hallmarks of the modern world – the progressive privatizing of religion and the emergence of a secular public sphere.[2]

In a world of growing religious plurality in which religious traditions did not have means to regain dominance or to create forms of peaceful coexistence there grew the conviction that religions should be freely practised but simultaneously that their public role in determining social, scientific and political reality should be greatly circumscribed. Reason, not religious traditions, would guide nations as they faced the modern world. As Jeffrey Stout has noted, a truce of sorts was formed, what he terms a pact of non-aggression, in which a universal reason common to all humans would govern the realm of cognition and knowledge, and religion and theology would hold sway in the arena of religious affectivity.[3] The implications of this pact were profound. Religion gained a continued safe place in the modern world but one that increasingly offered little justification for its public role. Religion, especially Christianity, became increasingly identified with the depths of human subjectivity, as in the work of the nineteenth-century Protestant theologian Friedrich Schleiermacher and the liberal theology to which he gave birth. A major repercussion of these intellectual, political and social shifts, scarcely envisioned by their original formulators, was that religion was increasingly viewed as what modern persons did in their newly configured private time, in the sphere of family and localized community.

Religious values and ideas certainly continued to influence public life but they did so with ever less legitimacy.

As religions' fortunes changed so too did the nature and role of theology. Theologians such as Schleiermacher formulated not only a new understanding of religion but also a drastically revised sense of what theology was about.[4] Far from being the articulator of timeless or absolute truth or the arbiter among competing claims, theology became a radically historicized mode of reflection in which theologians critically examined their traditions and sought to give expression to the convictions of those traditions in historically appropriate idioms. As such, theological claims changed over time and were relevant to particular traditions, but they were no longer universal in scope or absolute in intention. Thus, for a major strand of theology in the nineteenth century and beyond, religion had to do with the depth of human experience and theology became more and more focused on historically specific anthropology rather than larger cosmological or metaphysical claims. And while there were theological alternatives to these perspectives, such as neo-orthodoxy, such alternatives did little to alter the growing exclusion of religion's and theology's public function.

Other developments contributed to this de-centring of theology as well. One was the emergence of the modern university, epitomized by such institutions as the University of Berlin. The natural sciences grew in power in these institutions and the emerging social sciences sought to define themselves as disciplines with scientific stature, albeit characterized by methods appropriate to their human subjects. The place of theology in these settings was fiercely debated; sometimes theology and the training of clergy survived, as they did at Berlin, bolstered by the argument that the modern nation needed an educated clergy. Importantly, there emerged a growing 'science of religion' that sought to distinguish itself from all ecclesial authority and from confessional identification with religious communities. Hence, for example, the history of religion emerged at Göttingen, contrasting itself with the liberal but still Christian-centred vision of the Ritschlian School of Theology at the same institution. And in the Netherlands the Dutch Universities Act of 1876 established the sciences of religion within Dutch state universities and relegated dogmatic and practical theological disciplines to denominational seminaries. Broadly, there emerged a growing fascination with traditions and cultures other than western Christian and Jewish. In hindsight, such interests were clearly politically and ideologically fraught as western thinkers either denied that other cultures had a religion, or understood the religious status of the 'Other' as inferior to that of the

West, or negatively juxtaposed it to a superior western secularism.[5] Whatever the motivation, however, the West no longer existed in an isolated world and theology was no longer the self-evident climax of reflection about religion.

Within the United States the growing differentiation of the study of religion and theology unfolded in its own distinctive way. Here the relation of religion and the state has had a unique configuration and so, too, has the place of the study of religion and theology in higher education. In relation to the former, the American colonies were founded in significant part by the search for religious freedom. When the colonies rebelled in the eighteenth century against British rule the nation that was born sought both to protect the right to practise religion as a fundamental right and simultaneously asserted that the newly formed United States would have no established religion. These two impulses, religious freedom and the disestablishment of any state religion, have fuelled the debates and struggles over religion in America for more than two hundred years.

A significant outcome of the central commitment to a state and government not identified with a particular religion has been the separation of Church and state or, as was expressed by Thomas Jefferson (among others) in the early nineteenth century, the assertion that a wall of separation should exist between the state and all religions. This wall of separation has been embodied not only in relation to the government but, importantly, in how religion and its study have been understood in public education. For much of the history of the United States, religion was not studied in schools supported by the state or federal government. The study of religion was relegated to religiously identified divinity schools, seminaries and theological schools and to private educational institutions associated with religious bodies. Most often the religions studied were Christianity and Judaism. The other religious traditions of the world received scant attention. The goals of such study were, in graduate schools, the education of clergy and, in colleges and universities, the communication of the religious heritage of the founding denominations. The study of religion was, thus, deeply and positively connected with theology understood as an internal practice of a tradition, but both were disconnected from public education or, for the most part, from the examination of the full range of the world's religions. This separation reflected and contributed to the assumptions about the private nature of religious beliefs and practices that have so marked the modern world.

The current situation

In the United States a major sea change occurred in 1963 with the legal case of the School District of Abington v. Schempp. In this case, the Supreme Court ruled against the reading of Bible verses in public schools. However, in a concurring argument supporting the main ruling Justice Arthur Goldberg made the famous distinction between the teaching *of* religion and teaching *about* religion. This argument opened the door to the teaching of religion in publicly funded schools in the United States. In the aftermath of this ruling and out of growing cultural interest in other religions, numerous departments of religion and religious studies were founded in universities and colleges across America. These departments have been structured in a variety of ways and have embraced differing subjects of inquiry. But what they have increasingly shared in common has been the self-conscious exclusion of theology. Theology, once the dominant discipline within the divinity schools and theological schools that were the primary site of the analysis of religions, has increasingly found itself relegated *only* to those institutions and defined over against a now more academically legitimate study of religion. As Ray L. Hart noted, in his examination of the role of religious studies and theology in American higher education, scholars of religion offer diverse and conflicting accounts of their discipline but they increasingly share in common the assessment that what religious studies is *not* about is theology.[6] For a growing number of scholars in universities and colleges, theology has become part of the datum to be analysed rather than an accepted co-discipline in the study of religion. While theologians might represent the religious intellectuals of their traditions, their status as academically legitimate members of the academy has, in recent years, been greatly challenged. As departments of religious studies have proliferated and grown in stature, theology has been ever more marginalized and diminished as an academically esteemed enterprise.

A number of other factors more broadly related to our historical moment have intensified this situation. The development of the modern university has been accompanied by the emergence of distinctive disciplines and specializations. Scholars concentrate on ever more discrete subject matters and different areas of inquiry are characterized by distinctive methods, languages and modes of evaluation. The present-day university is not the site of unified or holistic interpretations of reality within which sub-fields are neatly arranged. Instead, the production of contemporary knowledge takes place in multiple locations with little interconnection. Even within places such as divinity or theological schools, the primary focus of which is one religious tradition, scholars and fields of study are frequently disconnected as historians, textualists, theologians and social scientists all work within their particular fields of inquiry or even their narrowly defined methodological approach to subject matters. Integration is often left to the individual student; it is not the outcome of a unified curriculum or shared approaches or content. Beyond theological schools such specialization is also the hallmark of the study of religion in general. This common phenomenon is illustrated by a quick perusal of the programmes of such organizations as the American Academy of Religion, and similar scholarly groups in Europe and elsewhere that testify to the fact that this is an era of specialized or narrowly conceived fields with little or no integration or even conversation across disciplinary lines. Thus not only are theology and religious studies in a state of disengagement but both are also characterized by endless subdivisions by subject matter, methods and ideology. It would, thus, be very difficult to gain agreement on just what the fields of religious studies and theology encompass today.

Specialization and the multiplication of fields of inquiry are not the only reasons for fragmentation and for the loss of any sense of unified or even broadly accepted knowledge. The modern period, especially in its Enlightenment mode, envisioned new forms of sure knowledge predicated not on the dictates of religion or ecclesial authority but on a publicly accessible and universally valid reason. But by the nineteenth century this vision was in the process of being challenged in profound ways, especially by the advent of historical consciousness. The recognition that the objects, persons and periods studied were all embedded in particular times and places was further complicated by the slowly dawning realization that scholars were also historical creatures, shaped by language, culture and power. An early proponent of the newly emergent discipline of history, Leopold von Ranke, argued that the task of the historian was to determine the mere facts and to do so by virtue of 'extinguishing' the self of the scholar.[7] By the end of the century and with ever greater force in the twentieth century, such notions of neutral scholars, unburdened by their own history or location, gave way to the understanding that all knowledge is situated and bears the imprint of its location. Both the Enlightenment's dream of unassailable knowledge and the nineteenth century's original hope of historically sensitive but still objective forms of understanding continued in many guises in the twentieth century. But their steady erosion has been the real legacy of the past century as modernity's illusions of objectivity and sure knowledge gave way to a postmodern sense of multiple truths and conflicting claims.

Accompanying this recognition of the value-and-power-laden character of knowledge have been further developments. It is also the case that in our current postmodern historical moment, in many instances our subject matters, our objects of inquiry, also appear as fragmented and multiple. What once seemed self-evident or obvious or unified has all fractured or dissolved into myriad forms. Culture, religion and the self – to name but a few – have lost their solidity and clear reference. Anthropologist Clifford Geertz expresses this when he speaks of the fleeting character of anthropology's most cherished concept – culture. He states: 'The trouble is no one is quite sure what culture is. Not only is it an essentially contested concept, like democracy, religion, simplicity, or social justice; it is fugitive, unsteady, encyclopedic, and normatively charged.'[8] Thus, both the knower and the objects of human inquiry are many, not one, not located above the historical fray and not purveyors of timeless meanings or truths, or neutral examiners of facts, but bearers of power, history and multiple possibilities.

Thus theology and its sibling discipline, religious studies, which often seeks to deny that they share a family of origin or are still positively related, both face a wider intellectual and social world in which the role, character and subject matter of academic inquiry is unclear and contested. Theology, in particular, occupies an unstable position, one far removed from its dominant position in the pre-modern world. How are we to conceive theology's identity today and what role can be imagined for theologians on the current scene?

Contemporary proposals

A number of different proposals have been articulated by theologians as they negotiate their positions in the academy, in relation to a sometimes hostile discipline of religious studies and in a wider historical moment distinguished by multiplicity, fragmentation and the contested character of all claims, including religious ones, to legitimacy and truth. Some, such as the recently emergent perspective 'radical orthodoxy', argue for a return to the pre-modern moment when an alternative, religiously charged world-view held sway.[9] In this view, the secular assumptions of both modernity and postmodernism would be challenged by the theologically structured interpretation of the world that developed at the assumed-to-be pinnacle of Christian development. Here theology re-emerges triumphantly both socially and in relation to academic disciplines like religious studies.

Post-liberalism, another contemporary interpretation of theology, suggests a somewhat different grounding for theology's current task.[10] It, too, rejects the Enlightenment's view of a universal, neutral reason that dominates all spheres of life. But it also turns away from the notions of universal experience or religious subjectivity that shaped the liberal tradition that developed in the nineteenth century. Instead, post-liberalism locates itself within present-day claims of the situated nature of all experience and thought. Post-liberals claim that theology, rather than articulating claims to universal truth or common human experience, is instead a form of reflection that takes place *within* the boundaries of particular religious traditions. Theology's task is to articulate tradition's central claims in contemporary form but equally importantly, to evaluate all beliefs and practices in terms of their faithfulness to the assumed-to-be core beliefs articulated in a tradition's central narratives. In this view, too, theology re-emerges in a powerful position; such a position is, however, not public, and is little related to religious studies or other academic disciplines. If in radical orthodoxy theology gains a new dominance, in post-liberalism it exists side by side with religious studies but without substantive engagement. Theology may be queen again but the kingdom has definitely become much smaller in scope.

A third option, which I term 'pragmatic historicism', has also been emerging.[11] From this perspective academic theology is interpreted as neither above religious studies or other disciplines nor side by side with them without critical engagement. Instead this view suggests theology, as it takes place in the academy, is a subset of religious studies whose task is to identify, critically engage and creatively reconfigure the meaning dimensions of religious traditions. This perspective is responsive to the growing awareness over the last century and a half of the historical, fallible, partial and located character of all human claims, including theological ones. It locates theology within those humanistic disciplines that seek to define and study what we have come to call religions and to explore the sources, meanings and functions of central beliefs or ideas and their relations to the wider dynamics of which they are a part. Theology, in this view, relinquishes its historic claim to dominance but equally rejects an isolationist role. It becomes one intellectual task among many, claiming its place alongside disciplines concerned with the analyses of other dimensions of religions such as texts, social function, rituals and practices etc. If it is no longer queen of the sciences, neither is theology the rejected former sibling. It is one intellectual partner among many, with an important but not elevated place in the academy. Neither queen nor unwelcome sibling, theology as a collegial voice among equals seems well suited to our age of fragmentation.

Notes

1. This essay is written from the perspective of a scholar who studies modern Protestant theology and especially American thought.
2. The modern split between the secular, public arena and a private, religious realm has long been assumed. However, the assumption that these are in simple opposition to each other is currently under great debate. See especially Jose Casanova, 1994, *Public Religions in the Modern World*, Chicago: University of Chicago Press and Talal Asad; 2003, *Formations of the Secular: Christianity, Islam and Modernity*, Stanford: Stanford University Press; and S. N. Balagangahara, 1993, *The 'Heathen in His Blindness...': Asia, the West and the Dynamics of Religion*, Leiden: Brill.
3. Jeffrey Stout, 1988, *Ethics after Babel: Languages of Morals and Their Discontents*, Boston: Beacon Press, p. 178.
4. See Friedrich Schleiermacher, 1976, *The Christian Faith*, trans. H. R. Mackintosh and J. S. Steward, Philadelphia: Fortress Press, pp. 88–9.
5. See especially David Chidester, 1996, *Savage Systems: Colonialism and Comparative Religion in Southern Africa*, Charlottesville: University of Virginia Press; Richard King, 1999, *Orientalism and Religion: Postcolonial Theory, India and 'the Mystic East'*, New York: Routledge; and Tomoko Masuzawa, 2005, *The Invention of World Religions: Or, How European Universalism was Preserved in the Language of Pluralism*, Chicago: University of Chicago Press.
6. Ray L. Hart, 1991, 'Religious and Theological Studies in American Higher Education', *Journal of the American Academy of Religion* 59:4.
7. See Leonard Krieger, 1977, *Ranke: the Meaning of History*, Chicago: University of Chicago Press, p. 5.
8. Clifford Geertz, 2000, *Available Light: Anthropological Reflections on Philosophical Topics*, Princeton: Princeton University Press, p. 11.
9. See John Milbank, Catherine Pickstock and Graham Ward, 1999, *Radical Orthodoxy: A New Theology*, London: Routledge.
10. See George A. Lindbeck, 1984, *The Nature of Doctrine: Religion and Theology in a Postliberal Age*, Philadelphia: Westminster Press.
11. See Sheila Greeve Davaney, 2000, *Pragmatic Historicism: A Theology for the Twenty-First Century*, Albany: State University of New York Press; 2006, *Historicism: The Once and Future Challenge to Theology*, Minneapolis: Fortress Press.

'Many Have Undertaken . . . and I too Decided': The One Story or the Many?

ELAINE WAINWRIGHT

Since *many have undertaken* to set down an orderly account of the events that have been fulfilled among us, just as they were handed on to us by those who from the beginning were eyewitnesses and servants of the word, *I too decided*, after investigating everything carefully from the very first, *to write an orderly account* for you, most excellent Theophilus, *so that you may know the truth* concerning the things about which you have been instructed. (Luke 1.1–4, NRSV)

This, the narrator's prologue to the Gospel of Luke, offers an insight into the process of story – or truth-telling – and meaning-making in relation to Jesus and the Jesus-event by one who was participant in that very process at its source. It recognizes the stages of gospel formation that were identified and highlighted by the Pontifical Biblical Commission's 1964 'Instruction on the Historical Truth of the Gospels, *Sancta Mater Ecclesia*,[1] namely, the life of Jesus ('events that have been fulfilled among us'), the testimony of the apostles ('those who from the beginning were eyewitnesses and servants of the word'), and the sacred authors (the 'many [who] have undertaken to set down an orderly account'). Like the Lukan narrator who claims 'the truth' (v. 4) for a particular account of the life of Jesus over against the other many accounts that have been undertaken, the Pontifical Biblical Commission in its 1964 document claims a unity and singularity of truth:

> In order to bring out with fullest clarity the enduring truth and authority of the Gospels, he [*sic*: the Catholic exegete] must, while carefully observing the rules of rational and of Catholic hermeneutics, make skillful use of the new aids to exegesis, especially those which the historical method, taken in its widest sense, has provided.[2]

The early Church, in its wisdom, did not consider the Lukan Gospel to be 'the truth' but rather included four different accounts of or perspectives on the life of Jesus in its canon. Adherents to Christian traditions within the contemporary world are likewise challenged by claims to a single 'enduring truth and authority' in a world context in which difference and differentiation have become hallmarks.[3] This has been manifest in biblical studies in which methodologies and hermeneutics have multiplied over the past two to three decades and hence diverse interpretations of biblical storytelling and meaning-making abound. This article will briefly examine these developments in light of the contribution a changed and changing discipline of biblical studies makes to Christian theologizing.

Shifting paradigms: methodological and hermeneutical

The above quote from the 1964 'Instruction on the Historical Truth of the Gospels, *Sancta Mater Ecclesia*' contains the Catholic Church's belated affirmation of the historical-critical method which had developed in Protestant biblical studies over previous centuries.[4] Historical criticism became the umbrella terminology for a variety of approaches that were textual, literary and historical and that were combined in a variety of ways in particular studies. It had an overall goal to establish the *intention of the original author* of a particular biblical text or texts in a historical context that was constructed using the best historical tools available at the particular time of the study.[5] While providing a wealth of information about biblical texts and contexts, the method was not readily accessible for preachers or communities of faith reading the Bible in the context of grass-roots theologizing.

In the last two decades of the twentieth century, there was an explosion of biblical methodologies and hermeneutics. The philosophies of Heidegger, Gadamer, Habermas and Ricoeur have highlighted, for many biblical scholars, the presuppositions that each one brings to the interpretation of texts from their location in particular contexts characterized by political, religious, socio-cultural and economic perspectives and influences.[6] The possibility of determining a value-neutral intention of an original author was questioned, and attention shifted from the world of the author behind the text to the world in front of the text created by meaning-making interpretation. Concerns over poverty, race, ethnicity, gender, culture, colonialism and ecology in the lives of biblical interpreters have given rise to an array of hermeneutical approaches: liberation, feminist, postcolonial, ecological and contextual.[7]

This has resulted, on the one hand, in a rich variety of biblical interpretations, even of the same text, together with a recognition of the different contexts in which church communities theologize (e.g. African churches facing the proliferation of HIV/AIDS). On the other hand, however, it has led to the development of enclaves of biblical interpretation such as African, Asian, feminist, postcolonial and others. This has strengthened the various streams of interpretation emerging from the recognition of difference and differentiation that characterized the second half of the twentieth century. There is a danger, however, of a fragmentation of biblical studies and its contribution to theology.[8] For the biblical scholar, however, this may not be seen as a danger when it is evident that biblical history, including early Christianity, was characterized by different communities of interpretation theologizing on their life situations in the light of their ongoing experience of God, of the life, death and resurrection of Jesus, and the implications of such theologizing for living in their diversity of contexts.[9]

It seems clear that different communities of interpretation today who are informed by particular concerns will interpret even the same text in different ways. I experienced this vividly just recently when a student in a post-graduate course, whose ethnic context is Maori, interpreted the story of the Canaanite woman of Matthew 15.21–28, a text for which I have offered a number of interpretations, in ways that differed significantly from any interpretation that I or others have given. Various contextual hermeneutics functioned within the inception of the biblical traditions in the same way that they function today in the interpretation of those traditions.

The development of diverse biblical methodologies in recent decades resulted not only from the hermeneutical shifts noted above but also from changes in the range of disciplines which inform ways of reading and interpreting texts: literary and rhetorical studies, social sciences and history itself. The social sciences and the new historicism, as they have been employed in biblical interpretation, have provided a 'thick' reconstruction of the contexts of biblical texts. The new literary and rhetorical studies have shifted the attention of many interpreters from the 'original author' to the text and its reader-centred meaning.[10] As a result of such a proliferation of approaches or methods, historical-critical studies have been nuanced and enhanced. Studies that use one of the newer approaches have developed the potentiality of the method. Other scholars have combined newer methodologies to develop approaches such as the socio-rhetorical.[11]

This diversification and specialization within current biblical studies was recognized and affirmed by the Pontifical Biblical Commission in its most recent statement 'Document on the Interpretation of the Bible in the Church',[12] suggesting that 'interdisciplinary collaboration will help overcome any limitations that specialization may tend to produce', a response which may seem initially to be a little simplistic.[13] The then Cardinal Joseph Ratzinger, in his preface to the document, did stress, however, the developmental nature of biblical interpretation, saying that '[t]he study of the Bible is ... never finished; each age must in its own way newly seek to understand the sacred books.'[14] One significant challenge today to such study is, indeed, the modes of differentiation and specialization that have informed biblical studies and that have the potential to fragment interpretation or to enrich and enliven the function of the biblical tradition within the churches.

Many still undertake to give an account

Just as the work of interpreting the Jesus story did not belong solely to the Lukan narrator, so too contemporary biblical interpretation does not belong to a single voice, be it that of church authorities, of biblical scholars, of church members or of the public in contemporary societies. Rather, it seems that more and more biblical scholars, especially those committed to the variety of contextual hermeneutics whose goal is transformation of Church and society (liberation, feminist, ecological, postcolonial and other named contextual perspectives), are finding themselves engaged with and among those who, from within the churches or the general public, are seeking to address critical ethical and moral challenges in today's world. Such issues include the act of making war on a sovereign state, the genderization of authority and leadership within the Catholic Church, the racial and ethnic face of poverty in various situations, the ordination of homosexual candidates within certain churches, the ravaging spread of HIV/AIDS in African and other Two-Thirds-World nations, and the many other major concerns that are engaging churches and societies. The interpretative work of engaged biblical scholars informed by the methodological and hermeneutical shifts noted above is being integrated into theological processes around the globe. It is to this that I now turn, aware that this shift is rebounding on the academy where the ethics of biblical interpretation[15] and the teaching and interpreting of the Bible in diverse contexts[16] are receiving significant attention.

Stephen Bevans in his *Models of Contextual Theology* has identified six different ways in which contemporary theologians and communities of faith are bringing the biblical tradition into dialogue with particular cultures and contexts.[17] His work reveals that understandings of the Bible itself differ among theologians or communities using the various models. Those who use the Translation Model, for instance, believe that it is possible to separate the gospel message from its cultural articulation. Within models such as the Praxis, Synthetic and Transcendental, there is recognition that the Bible is culturally conditioned and hence incomplete. It needs, therefore, ongoing interpretation in new cultural or contextual situations. The Praxis Model, in particular, especially as it has functioned within liberation theology, assumes that interpretation of Scripture can be undertaken by all readers.[18] The recently published *Global Bible Commentary* referred to above provides brief commentaries on biblical books from a variety of methodological approaches. It reveals the different perspectives on the Bible and its relation to culture that are functioning within contextual theologizing. What is clear is that as biblical interpretation moves from the control of its dominant practitioners who have been white, western, male, academic and in many instances clerical, to contexts in which scholars from a range of locations are engaged with grass-roots readers in praxis toward transformation, interpretations have become diverse.

Feminist biblical interpretation is one example of such a shift and over the last three decades a wide range of feminist biblical interpretations using all of the newer methodologies have appeared.[19] Feminism shares with other movements for transformation the fragmenting potential of differentiation within current biblical studies, including feminist biblical studies. Elisabeth Schüssler Fiorenza has been one of the foremothers of contemporary feminist biblical interpretation and one of its key practitioners over the past thirty years. In her recent book *Wisdom Ways*, directed not only to academics but to the Bible reader generally, she invites them 'to probe and engage the possibilities for articulating a feminist biblical spirituality that sustains rather than mutes struggles for self-esteem, survival, and transformation'.[20] With this as the goal, Schüssler Fiorenza then proposes a way of engaging readers in what she calls the 'twirling, moving, spiraling dance of feminist biblical interpretation'.[21] There will, therefore, be difference and differentiation because of the different locations of women undertaking feminist biblical interpretation, but the goal of transformation is what can unite women, and varied biblical interpretations can serve the goal. Both interpretations and action for change can be and must be continually tested in light of the goal. Is each interpretation ethical in terms of the perspective and action it authorizes? This points, therefore, to the testing of interpretations in a context of differentiation; and ethics within a transformational perspective is one way of undertaking such testing.[22]

The final example I wish to offer to this discussion is that proposed by

Daniel Patte with Monya A. Stubbs, Justin Ukpong and Revelation E. Velunta in *The Gospel of Matthew: A Contextual Introduction for Group Study*. They propose a three-tiered approach 'through a set of roundtable discussions' whose goal is 'not to reach a conclusion about which interpretation is the best in all circumstances, but to recognize that which is best in a particular situation to particular people'.[23] Patte calls this approach 'scriptural criticism', or in another context, 'reading with'.[24] As with the approach of feminist biblical interpretation, so too scriptural criticism seeks to be ethically accountable to its goal of transformation, the work of all committed to biblical liberation, not just of academics.

Conclusion

Examining movements and developments in biblical studies over the past three decades has revealed that, like other areas of human endeavour, it too has become both more specialized and differentiated. A wide range of new practitioners, both academic and grass roots, have entered the field; proliferation of methodologies and hermeneutics has led to increased specialization; and hermeneutics with social and cultural transformation as a goal has brought academics and grass-roots interpreters together in ways that are challenging both churches and society. There are a variety of ways in which the various interpretations emerging from this differentiation might be tested. Even though each interpreter does not necessarily share the perspective which recognizes a wide range of interpretations within the biblical text, there is, however, significant acceptance of the premise that diversity in contemporary interpretation can be seen as biblical. It is this insight together with its multiplicity of interpretations which biblical studies contributes to contemporary theology.

Notes

1. Pontifical Biblical Commission, 2002, 'Instruction on the Historical Truth of the Gospels, *Sancta Mater Ecclesia*', in *The Scripture Documents: An Anthology of Official Catholic Teachings*, ET Dean P. Béchard (ed.), Collegeville: Liturgical Press, pp. 227–35.
2. Pontifical Biblical Commission, 'Instruction', p. 228, para. IV.
3. The centrality of difference or differentiation in postmodern consciousness is widely attested. See, for example, Rosi Braidotti, 1991, *Patterns of Dissonance*, New York: Routledge; and, 1994, *Nomadic Subjects: Embodiment and Sexual*

Difference in Contemporary Feminist Theory, New York: Columbia University Press.

4. Alexa Suelzer and John S. Kselman, 'Modern Old Testament Criticism', and John S. Kselman and Ronald D. Witherup, 'Modern New Testament Criticism', in *The Jerome Biblical Commentary*, ed. Raymond E. Brown, Joseph A. Fitzmyer and Roland E. Murphy (Englewood Cliffs: Prentice Hall, 1990, pp. 1113–29 and 1130–45), provide a brief overview of the development of this method. Its gradual affirmation in the Catholic Church during the early twentieth century is outlined in Joseph Cardinal Ratzinger's introduction to the Pontifical Biblical Commission's 1993 'Document on the Interpretation of the Bible in the Church', in *The Scripture Documents: An Anthology of Official Catholic Teachings*, ed. and trans. Dean P. Béchard, Collegeville: Liturgical Press, 2002, p. 245.

5. Edgar Krentz, 1975, *The Historical-Critical Method* (Philadelphia: Fortress Press) provides a succinct description of the method.

6. See David Jasper, 2004, *A Short Introduction to Hermeneutics*, Louisville: Westminster John Knox Press, pp. 99–118.

7. For two collections which demonstrate these approaches, see Susanne Scholz, 2003, *Biblical Studies Alternatively: An Introductory Reader*, Upper Saddle River: Prentice Hall; and Daniel Patte et al., 2004, *Global Bible Commentary*, Nashville: Abingdon Press.

8. This is one of the concerns which informs L. William Countryman, 2003, *Interpreting the Truth: Changing the Paradigm of Biblical Studies*, Harrisburg: Trinity Press International, p. 1.

9. S. E. Gillingham, 1998, *One Bible, Many Voices: Different Approaches to Biblical Studies*, London: SPCK, pp. 27–45.

10. An example of the variety of methodologies which have emerged is found in Steven L. McKenzie and Stephen R. Haynes (eds), 1999, *To Each Its Own Meaning: An Introduction to Biblical Criticisms and Their Application*, rev. edn, Louisville: Westminster John Knox Press.

11. See for instance Vernon K. Robbins, 1996, *Exploring the Texture of Texts: A Guide to Socio-Rhetorical Interpretation*, Valley Forge: Trinity Press International.

12. Pontifical Biblical Commission, 'Document on the Interpretation of the Bible in the Church', pp. 244–317.

13. Pontifical Biblical Commission, 'Document on the Interpretation of the Bible in the Church', p. 297.

14. Pontifical Biblical Commission, 'Document on the Interpretation of the Bible in the Church', p. 244.

15. Elisabeth Schüssler Fiorenza, 1990, *Rhetoric and Ethic: The Politics of Biblical Interpretation*, Minneapolis: Fortress Press; Daniel Patte, 1995, *Ethics of Biblical Interpretation: A Reevaluation*, Louisville: Westminster/John Knox

Press; and Elna Mouton, 2002, *Reading a New Testament Document Ethically*, Atlanta: Society of Biblical Literature.
16. This is manifest in recent additions to the annual programme of the Society of Biblical Literature, e.g. 'Teaching the Bible in Racially and Culturally Diverse Classrooms', 'Latino/a Approaches to the Bible', 'Contextual Biblical Interpretation', 'Ecological Hermeneutics' and 'Theological Hermeneutics of Christian Scripture Group'.
17. Stephen B. Bevans, 2004, *Models of Contextual Theology*, rev. and expanded edn, Maryknoll: Orbis Books.
18. Bevans, *Models*, pp. 141–3, provides a summary of the six models considered. Detailed discussion of the various models is the content of the book.
19. Some of this variety is manifest in two commentaries which, in feminist biblical studies, could be compared with the *Global Bible Commentary*, namely, Carol A. Newsom and Sharon H. Ringe (eds), 1992, *The Women's Bible Commentary*, expanded edn, Louisville: Westminster/John Knox Press; and Elisabeth Schüssler Fiorenza (ed.), 1994, *Searching the Scriptures: Volume 2 – A Feminist Commentary*, New York: Crossroad.
20. Elisabeth Schüssler Fiorenza, 2001, *Wisdom Ways: Introducing Feminist Biblical Interpretation*, Maryknoll: Orbis Books, p. 2.
21. Schüssler Fiorenza, *Wisdom Ways*, p. 18. See p. 194 for a diagram of the dance of interpretation proposed by Schüssler Fiorenza.
22. Sandra M. Schneiders, 1999, *The Revelatory Text: Interpreting the New Testament as Sacred Scripture* (Collegeville: Liturgical Press, pp.164–7), offers some general criteria for testing interpretations in a context of multiplication and differentiation of methodological approaches and hermeneutical perspectives.
23. Daniel Patte with Monya A. Stubbs, Justin Ukpong and Revelation E. Velunta, 2003, *The Gospel of Matthew: A Contextual Introduction for Group Study*, Nashville: Abingdon, p. 14.
24. Daniel Patte, 'Introduction', in *Global Bible Commentary*, pp. xxix–xxxii.

Theological Ethics without Theology? Assessing Theological-Ethical Reflection of Moral Challenges Posed by Pluralism in Relation to Theology

CHRISTOPH BAUMGARTNER

Since its beginning as an independent discipline at the end of the sixteenth century Catholic moral theology, or theological ethics, has developed in a way that has led to a situation which is distinctively different from its origin. Whereas its beginning lies in the context of the confessional practice and in the discussion of specific cases of problems of conscience that were related to this practice,[1] moral theology today can be described as a theological discipline that, in the light of the Christian understanding of the world and of all humanity, reflects on the right and proper behaviour of all human beings in all areas of life. The focus is no longer on explicitly religious actions such as the confessional practice. Nowadays these are issues for other theological disciplines such as pastoral theology or religious education. This process of change within moral theology, or rather theological ethics, can also be seen in the light of its research methodology. The scientific academic character of theology in general, and the demands resulting from this, require of modern theological ethics an interdisciplinary methodology. This is particularly true for the analysis and assessment of specific moral problems, as in 'special moral teaching' or rather in so-called 'applied ethics', where results from the humanities and social sciences are reviewed as well as those of natural sciences and medicine. As it will be shown, this approach is necessary in order to be able to reflect adequately on the moral challenges related to the pluralistic world-views of modern environments and those which are posed by modern technologies.

One result of this development within the subject is the tendency to change the name of this theological sub-discipline in which the reflection on the right and proper action is done. Here the term 'theological ethics' has found its place beside 'moral theology'. This mirrors a tendency of ethics 'becoming institutionally independent'[2] within the canon of theological disciplines; a tendency which is, however, true also for other disciplines. Rather, the development of moral theology, or theological ethics as I have described it here, has to be viewed in the larger context of a growing specialization in many sciences in general and in theology in particular, as well as in the context of an increasing differentiation of the diverse sub-disciplines which is a consequence of this specialization. These diverse disciplines of theology differ substantially not only in the methods they use but also in the questions they address and in their objects of research. Hence a specialization and differentiation within theology is sometimes viewed as a danger to the unity of theology. There is a further aspect which has to be looked at individually but still cannot be separated from this issue. It is a question regarding the above mentioned tendency to specialize and 'to become independent' which applies to a number of disciplines within theology. Does this tendency in the case of ethics not also lead to a tendency of 'de-theologizing'? If we look at the development which from the end of the sixteenth century has changed and modified moral theology to theological ethics, has this process led this discipline out of and away from theology? In what follows we will describe as the 'de-theologization thesis' the tendency inherent in theology to fragment into several theological subdisciplines, which in the case of ethics also implies a tendency to 'de-theologize'. If one examines this thesis a little closer, it becomes apparent that it shows a number of aspects which are important for its discussion and assessment. Thus it simply speaks of 'theology' without any further explanation as to what is meant by this term. Speaking of an inner tendency of theology to split into several subdisciplines, however, suggests that we are referring to theology as an academic discipline. It is nevertheless essential to define the concept of theology more precisely to be able to decide whether the above thesis is in fact sustainable, whether we can indeed speak of theological ethics being 'de-theologized'. In addition, the formulation of the thesis leaves open how a possible process of de-theologizing ought to be assessed and if, in terms of evaluation, it is relevant at all.

In what follows, these aspects will be discussed in different ways, while the main focus of interest will remain on the question of a possible de-theologization of theological ethics. For this I will proceed in three steps. First, I will introduce a certain understanding and concept of theology which will be the background for the third step where I will discuss and assess the thesis proposed above. In between these two steps, that is, the introduction of a concept of theology and the discussion of the de-theologization thesis, I will make a few short remarks concerning a certain model of ethics that tries to reflect methodologically adequately on the moral challenges posed by modern, pluralistic societies.

Which theology?[3]

There are a number of possible definitions for the term 'theology'. The original meaning of the word was simply 'speaking about God'. This includes some very different ways of speaking, such as preaching or narrative speaking about God, as well as the academic, scientific reflection about God. It does not become much clearer even if we narrow the term 'theology' down to denote theology as an academic discipline. Worldwide, theology currently appears as an academic subject in such a great and diverse number of versions that it seems impossible from the start to define a universally valid understanding of theology that would be sufficiently concrete and specific to discuss and assess the previously proposed thesis. David Ford, for example, presents a rather general description: 'Theology [. . .] is thinking about questions raised by and about religions.'[4] Peter Eicher is only slightly more precise in his Introduction to the new edition of *Neues Handbuch theologischer Grundbegriffe*. There he describes the classic task of theology as 'to strive for an academic understanding of the living and lived religion and to provide a critical assessment of the religion's pragmatic contribution to the concrete situation of the world in which we live'.[5]

So which concept of theology should be used as a basis to discuss and analyse the 'de-theologization thesis'? It is certainly reasonable to choose a model that on the one hand is to a large extent representative for at least the majority of international theologians. On the other hand, it should be formulated in a way that is 'fruitful' for discussing the question of this article in the sense that it poses a real challenge and it does not rule out an open analysis and assessment of the 'de-theologization thesis' right from the start.[6] Both conditions are fulfilled by the model of 'theology as the science of faith'. This model can be described as follows.[7] The object of this form of theology is formally God or rather the world and human beings in view of God and God's history with human beings. In addition, the object of research of this type of theology is the (Christian) faith. However, faith is here not only the object of theological research but at the same time its fundament and basis. Theology as science of faith comes, as it were, out of the (Christian) faith and begins from there. It aims at a rational understanding and also at a critical reflection of faith. Thus theology 'has the Christian faith in a subjective and objective perspective as its precondition, fundament, object and aim. It is therefore participant and theoretical companion of the faith at the same time.'[8] Accordingly, for theology to be science in this sense it has to comply with certain relevant standards of rationality, such as the aiming for insights which are inter-subjective and rationally comprehensible. Theology also has to obey the rules of argumentative, scientific discourse. In doing so, theologians accept the view that science is historically determined and conditioned and, with this, the necessity for change in the practice of science. From this follows a 'commandment for the scientific constitution of theology to be in keeping with the times'.[9]

Ethics as a theological discipline in view of the challenge of pluralism[10]

Generally speaking, ethics is the academic reflection of human behaviour and action, of moral norms, attitudes and views, as well as the reflection of social institutions from the perspective of what is good and right.[11] In the case of theological ethics this reflection of good and proper action is done within the Christian understanding of the world and of human beings, in other words, it is done within the 'Christian horizon of meaning and sense'.[12]

This rather general definition leaves room for quite different forms of ethics. In fact, to speak of 'theological ethics' is impossible. The same restrictions apply here which make it impossible and meaningless to speak of 'theology' as such. With regard to some ethical concepts that are relevant in the context of theology, the de-theologization thesis has to be clearly rejected. This is true, for example, for concepts that have been developed in the framework of liberation theology and under recourse to Emmanuel Levinas. In general, here the concepts are explicitly linked with convictions of faith or religious experiences. An analysis of modern representative handbooks on theological ethics also shows that we cannot speak of a de-theologization of ethics throughout theology in general. Thus in the international field, the *Oxford Handbook of Theological Ethics* (2005), edited by Gilbert Meilaender and William Werpehowski, shows an explicitly theological structure.

The situation is less clear with models of theological ethics that attempt a systematic reflection of good and proper human action within the framework of the ideological pluralism characteristic of numerous liberal societies. This 'fact of pluralism' (John Rawls) is combined with a multitude of diverse and partly conflicting ways of life. One attempt to solve the problems arising from this situation is to distinguish between questions concerning a good life and questions of justice, or rather the distinction between a perspective of ethics concerned with striving and ethics focusing on norms.[13] For years, the exact determination of the relation between the good and the just or the proper has been the object of controversial debates. The position which will be sketched out in the following, and which forms the basis for the reflections to come, follows essentially a liberal view because through such a position the questions related to the de-theologization thesis become particularly evident.

At the heart of the ethics of 'ambition' (Strebeusethik) is the quest for a good and successful life. Evaluative statements in the context of an ethics of ambition depend on specific concepts of 'the good'. Hence they have the character of suggestions and recommendations. Still, what various individuals and groups consider as good ways of life for themselves need not necessarily be seen as equally desirable for everybody nor can it be justified as such for all. This necessitates the perspective of 'the just or proper' as a view distinct from the ethics of ambition and as the perspective of prime importance. This is the object of the ethics of 'obligation' (Sollensethik). Ethical statements in this context – moral norms in the narrow sense – are strictly normative, and, in contrast to ethical statements in the context of an ethics of ambition, these norms claim universal and categorical validity. Accordingly, each person must give priority to norm-ethical rules in his or her actions. Against the good of the ethics of ambition, the 'morally right' of the ethics of obligation claims a systematic priority.

Like philosophical ethics, theological ethics aims for the formulation and justification of criteria for the good and the right. However, philosophical and theological ethics differ in so far as theological ethics reflects human action against a Christian horizon of meaning and on the basis of Christianity's understanding of the world and human beings. This is based on the fundamental conviction of Christianity that what has been revealed in faith is of particular relevance for the action and acting of all human beings. It is a conviction that is clearly expressed in Jesus' proclamation of the Kingdom of God and his call to practical repentance. Yet, for a model that follows the model sketched out above, this concrete and practical function of the Christian horizon of sense is not automatically obvious. In the field of the ethics of ambition, a certain methodological connection with some elements of the Christian faith is certainly possible. Thus, for example, models of a good life could be built on, and orientated on, the imitation of Jesus.

Concerning the ethics of obligation, we have to distinguish between the context of discovery and the context of reason.[14] As far as it concerns the area of discovery and of acquiring insights which are relevant for the just, the Christian world-view and understanding of human beings can perfectly well have a special function. Thus, for example, the Christian framework of meaning and sense can provide a critical perspective which critically analyses in each case the dominant moral and which opens a view beyond the 'ethical minimum'. It is also here that the question about the place of the moral in the context of the whole of human life is raised. Alfons Auer has called this the 'integrating, criticizing and stimulating effect of the Christian horizon of meaning' for the process of finding moral norms.[15]

Christianity claims that it has a message for all people. This implies that insights *discovered* in the light of the Christian view of the world and its people cannot form a 'specifically religious morality'. In addition, it is impossible to use directly convictions of faith for argumentative foundation of principles and norms in the context of an ethics of obligation. For this, we must justify moral norms which are valid and binding in the same way for everyone. Consequently they must be valid also for followers of different religious and non-religious world-views. For a crucial function of such norms is that they enable a peaceful and just life together of people whose world-view and concepts of a good life differ and are in conflict with each other. Therefore, obligation-ethical norms must fulfil certain demands such as autonomy and an argumentative foundation beyond the boundaries of specific groups or communities of faith. The pluralism of world-views means that we cannot assume that religious convictions are shared and accepted by those answerable to obligation-ethical norms. Hence, such conviction cannot form the main force in the discourse on the argumentative foundation of such norms. Consequently, theological ethics which follows the model sketched out above argues in this area in such a way that its basic force of argument and conviction does not depend on revealed truths and other (exclusively) religious or theological convictions.[16]

Theological ethics – de-theologized?

The previous section has presented a rough sketch of a concept of theological ethics which tries to do justice to the challenges of pluralism as described before. If we take this as a starting point to assess the de-theologization thesis, this thesis appears to have a certain plausibility. One central issue of theological ethics is the formulation and justification of obligation-ethical principles and norms. If in this field theological ethics becomes virtually indistinguishable[17] from philosophical ethics, is it then not justified to speak of 'de-theologization' of ethics? Whereas in the model of theology as science of faith the Christian faith is not only the precondition but also the object and aim of theology, it seems that in theological ethics that follow the 'liberal' paradigm sketched out above, the Christian faith no longer has an essential role to play. Josef Schuster describes the problem that seems related to such an interpretation by highlighting that on the one hand the 'offer of current philosophy and ethics' described above might enable us with the problem of pluralism with the prospect of some success; on the other hand,

> for moral theology it contains the inherent danger of being relegated into the private realm of a particular attitude intrinsically linked with a specific world-view and so merely sustaining a group ethos which at best would be relevant for Christians but which would no longer address 'all people of good will'. Yet, if moral theology wants to constitute itself as a pure theory of justice, it is in danger of losing its essential characteristic: the relation with the Christian faith and its centre Jesus Christ.[18]

However, to interpret in such a way the concept of theological ethics as it is described above and an acceptance of the 'de-theologization thesis' that might result from this ignores in my view essential aspects of theological ethics which follows the programme of distinguishing between the good (ethics of ambition) and the just (ethics of obligation) and the methodological consequences that result from it. I will briefly explain this in the following. Before doing so, however, I emphasize again that the following discussion analyses only a certain model of theological ethics in the light of which the de-theologization thesis seems to have a certain initial plausibility. As I have said already before, this does not apply to other concepts of theological ethics in the same way. This also includes those concepts which conceive the relation between the good and the just differently from the way it has been described above.[19]

All this might suggest an initial plausibility of the de-theologization thesis in view of a certain form of theological ethics. This is connected with the fact that in this form of ethics norm-ethical principles and norms are formulated and argued in a way which mentions neither God nor the Christian faith explicitly. At first sight this seems virtually incompatible with the model described above, of theology as science of faith. However, such a renunciation of explicitly religious convictions in the context of the formulating and rationalization of obligation-ethical principles and rules should not be understood as 'de-theologization'. On the contrary, this should be perceived as a specific method which indeed enables theological ethics at all to make a contribution as theological ethics to solve the moral problems posed by free and liberal societies which are pluralistic in their world-views. As I have already said, the Christian faith claims to present a message relevant for the actions of all people. One of the tasks of theological ethics is to unfold the practical implications of the Christian view of the world and human beings within scientific and academic discourse. For this, theological ethics, according to the concept of theology as science of faith, understands itself as being obliged to the relevant standards in science of each historical situation. The 'commandment that the academic constitution of theology has to be in keeping with the times' (Max Seckler; ET: TH) contains also the call for a methodology that does justice to each object of research and to the current state of academic and scientific discourse. To do justice to its object of research the exegesis of the twenty-first century *as a matter of necessity* uses methods different from those of scholastic exegesis (including, not least, some methods whose origin does not lie in theology).[20] Likewise, theological ethics must also work with a methodology that enables us to expect a relevant contribution to the scientific analysis and assessment of current moral challenges. In the case of the obligation-ethical dimension of ethics this is mirrored in a type of language which is not explicitly, and even less exclusively, theological. This, however, is no 'de-theologization', rather it is done for the sake of the cause of Christianity and it corresponds in this sense to the understanding of theology as science of faith.

It is undisputed that, influenced by the development (and to some extent also by the diversification) of the concept of science and also through the dialogue with other disciplines, theology as a whole has continuously developed further its own identity as a subject and the way it sees itself.[21] Theological ethics is also involved in this process. The object of theological ethics is human action. The contexts for human action are becoming increasingly diverse and pluralistic. This is why the formal object of theology as science of faith (God or the world and human beings in view of God and his history with the people) is perhaps indeed not immediately obvious in some discourses in which theological ethics is involved. However, this does not mean that within an increasingly differentiated theology ethics is becoming 'de-theologized'. On the contrary, facing the methodological challenges posed to ethical discourse by current issues and problems is rather a necessary condition for theology to make any contribution to reflection on and assessment of the moral problems of the present time. Therefore it is possible that (in some discourses) theologians do not refer to God or the Christian faith *explicitly*, but still, in this sense, theological ethics can be and remain a theological discipline. Moreover, to formulate and reason out moral principles and norms which claim to be universally and categorically valid (ethics of obligation), this is even methodologically appropriate. Finally, attention should be drawn to developments within political philosophy which indicate that within the ethics of obligation theological ethics can make its own contribution, even though this may be limited. Authors such as John Rawls and Jürgen Habermas have pointed out in their publications that the practical acceptance of universally compulsory, moral principles and norms depends on the citizens being able to integrate such norms into the fundamental convictions of their world-view. Rawls has formulated this in his concept of 'broad public reason'.[22] On the other hand, Habermas (building on Rawls) writes in the context of religious tolerance that the great religions must express the basic norms of liberal states in their own formulae, and thereby embed the universally binding moral elements into their respective convictions of faith. Accordingly, we ought to speak of the justification, or rather of the making plausible, of such norms as a process in two steps. As a first step, universally valid, moral norms must be justified with arguments which are convincing for all people involved regardless of their convictions of faith. Then, in a second step, an attempt is made to guarantee practical loyalty to the moral norms by embedding them in the respective world-view of the addressees involved. While the first step of reasoning has to be done by ethics using the philosophical method of arguing, the second step must argue with explicit recourse to specific convictions of faith. Yet, Habermas highlights in no uncertain terms that (in view of universally valid norms) the second step has to give preference to the right in contrast to the good in the sense described above: 'In many cases this [developing the normative principles of the secular order from within the view of a respective religious tradition and community] makes it necessary to revise attitudes and prescriptions that (as with the dogmatic prejudice against homosexuality for example) claim support from a long-standing tradition of interpretations of holy scriptures.'[23]

In this sense we could speak of a task of 'the critical evaluation of religion' which theological ethics would be called to fulfil *ad intra*, that is to say this task would have to be done in view of its own community of faith, and its faith. This task would complement the view that the function of theological ethics, according to Alfons Auer, is to provide a critical perspective to universally held moral norms. At this point a renewed consideration of the model of theology as science of faith proves to be instructive. There are two directions of criticism: one inward-looking towards the concrete faith of one's own community of faith but also towards theology itself; the other outward-looking towards the 'world', also in the sense of concrete institutions of society. Max Seckler names both directions as essential areas of work for theology.[24] Against this background there seems to be perhaps even an indication that a serious engaging with the challenges that are connected with the pluralism of world-views does not lead ethics out of theology, but, on the contrary, that this could in a sense lead to a strengthening of the identity of theology.

Translated by Thomas Höbel.

Notes

1. See J. Theiner, 1970, *Die Entwicklung der Moraltheologie zur eigenständigen Disziplin*, Regensburg.
2. See H.-J. Birkner, 1993, 'Das Verhältnis von Dogmatik und Ethik', in A. Hertz et al. (eds), *Handbuch der christlichen Ethik*, vol. 1, Freiburg i. Br.: Herder, pp. 281–96, here p. 282 (ET: TH).
3. For the following, see W. Kasper, 1988, 'Die Wissenschaftspraxis der Theologie', in W. Kern, H. J. Pottmeyer and M. Seckler (eds), *Handbuch der Fundamentaltheologie*, vol. IV, Freiburg i. Br.: Herder, pp. 242–77. See also in particular M. Seckler, 1988, 'Theologie als Glaubenswissenschaft', in Kern, Pottmeyer and Seckler (eds), *Handbuch der Fundamentaltheologie*, pp. 179–241.
4. D. Ford, 1999, *Theology: A Very Short Introduction*, Oxford and New York: Oxford University Press.
5. P. Eicher, 2005, 'Vorwort', in *Neues Handbuch theologischer Grundbegriffe*, vol. I, Munich, pp. 7–15 (ET: TH).
6. This, for example, would be the case with a very broad understanding of theology that includes the analysis of religious and cultural occurrences in a very broad sense. Against the background of such an understanding of theology a confirmation of the de-theologization thesis is obviously not to be expected.
7. See Seckler, 'Glaubenswissenschaft', pp. 179–241.
8. Seckler, 'Glaubenswissenschaft', p. 196.
9. Seckler, 'Glaubenswissenschaft', p. 201 (ET: TH). According to Seckler, a further characteristic element of theology as science of faith is its ecclesial dimension. From this perspective the de-theologization thesis could be understood as a thesis of 'un-churching'. However, this question and, related to it, the

debate of clarifying the relation between academic theology and ecclesial authority cannot be discussed here.

10. For the following, see in particular M. Düwel, C. Hübenthal and M. H. Werner (eds), 2002, *Handbuch Ethik*, Stuttgart/Weimar; H. Haker, 1999, *Moralische Identität. Literarische Lebensgeschichten als Medium ethischer Reflexion*, Tübingen; H. Krämer, 1992, *Integrative Ethik*, Frankfurt am Main; C. Mandry, 2002, *Ethische Identität und christlicher Glaube. Theologische Ethik im Spannungsfeld von Theologie und Philosophie*, Mainz; D. Mieth, 2005, 'Ethik. A. Aus katholischer Sicht', in P. Eicher (ed.), *Neues Handbuch theologischer Grundbegriffe*, vol. I, Munich, pp. 282–93.
11. See Mieth, 'Ethik', p. 282.
12. See A. Auer, 1984, *Autonome Moral und christlicher Glaube*, 2nd, expanded edn, Düsseldorf.
13. For the distinction between the good and the right in ethics, see in particular Krämer, *Integrative Ethik*; J. Rawls, 1993, *Political Liberalism*, Lecture V, New York. For the discussion of the above mentioned distinction from a theological perspective, see also Haker, *Identität*, and E. Mack, 2002, *Gerechtigkeit und gutes Leben. Ethik im politischen Diskurs*, Paderborn.
14. For the difference between the context of discovery and that of reason see D. Mieth, 1998, *Moral und Erfahrung II*, Freiburg (CH).
15. Auer, *Autonome Moral*, pp. 185ff. (ET: TH). The Christian concept of meaning has not only a certain influence on the acquiring of morally relevant insights, it also influences the motivation for acting morally. For this, see Auer, *Autonome Moral*, pp. 177ff. See also Baumgartner, 2005, *Umweltethik – Umwelthandeln. Ein Beitrag zur Lösung des Motivationsproblems*, Paderborn.
16. However, this is not to say that arguments presented in the discourse of reasoning and argumentative foundation are completely 'detached' from religious convictions. These rather retain their specific context within the convictions of those involved in the discourse. See also Mandry, *Ethische Identität*.
17. The theory of 'differentiation through non-difference' has been formulated in the context of the theological ethics of Dietmar Mieth. Mieth refers here in particular to the *theologoumenon* of the incarnation and to the writings of Meister Eckhart. For this, see D. Mieth, 1982, 'Autonomie der Ethik – Neutralität des Evangeliums?', *Concilium* 18, pp. 320–7, here particularly pp. 325ff.
18. J. Schuster, 2005, 'Fragen des guten Lebens und Fragen der Gerechtigkeit. Anmerkungen zu einer Unterscheidung und deren Konsequenzen', *Trierer Theologische Zeitschrift* 114, pp. 116–28, here p. 118 (ET: TH).
19. Just to mention in passing: theological-ethical models are often far less liberalistic than the model presented above, which has been put forward in a particularly clear-cut way for the sake of discussing the de-theologization thesis. On the contrary, theological-ethical debates usually do not see ethics of ambition

and ethics of obligation as separate from each other, but rather as related to each other. For this, see for example the works of Hille Hacker and Christof Mandry mentioned above.
20. See Seckler, 'Glaubenswissenschaft', p. 201.
21. See A. Fortin-Melkevik, 1994, 'Die Methoden der Theologie und interdisziplinäres Denken', *Concilium* 30, pp. 546–53.
22. See J. Rawls, 1997, 'The Idea of Public Reason Revisited', *The University of Chicago Law Review* 564 (1997), pp. 765–807.
23. J. Habermas, 2004, 'Religious Tolerance – the Pacemaker for Cultural Rights', *Philosophy* 79, pp. 5–18, here p. 13.
24. Seckler, 'Glaubenswissenschaft', pp. 237ff. Also, as formulated by Habermas that, if need be, certain morally relevant attitudes and prescriptions of a religion must be re-examined and revised in the light of moral insights, is a claim that can be defended within the framework of Seckler's concept of theology as science of faith and the relation of reason and revelation contained therein: 'the principle that ultimately reason and revelation cannot be in contradiction to each other is true for both directions. It demands in cases of conflict a re-examination of our knowledge based on reason and of our faith based on revelation which are both of a historical and contingent kind' (p. 195). However, it should be noted that Habermas's example of certain attitudes towards homosexuality must not be understood as part of the faith of revelation.

Church History without God or without Faith?

WILLEM FRIJHOFF

The use and the necessity of writing history

When the Church, of whichever denomination, still had the monopoly on the social embedding of faith in God, it was taken for granted that God was present in church history as a given. The uniqueness of God was reflected in the assurance/certainty that there was only *one* possible history of the Church, that is, the one which ultimately – in spite of all human failures and errors, in spite of all manner of apostasy, heresy or abuse of power – would recount the story of the success of the one true Church. Whether Catholic or Protestant, the Church saw the fundamental legitimization of its historical development confirmed in the unity of throne and altar, of nation and community of faith, of Church and state. A flourishing society was not only a Christian society, but a society in which the institutional Church appeared as the guardian of faith and as the umpire/judge of good and evil. Then Christendom became gradually more and more divided into a multiplicity of churches, ecclesial communities, confessions, independent groups, even autonomous congregations. Initially, this did not destroy the sense of the social affirmation of being the elect and of being in agreement with the revealed truth. As long as the church community was able to refer to God being visibly on its side, it had the confidence to be able to develop in the direction it desired, if necessary even against the entire world. Even today there are clear examples for this kind of thinking. Let us just think of the communities of the Old Order in the United States of America which have withdrawn from the world. The best-known example among them are the Anabaptist Amish People.[1] The same, however, applies to the world-affirming Christian fundamentalism which today is central to the agenda of the mainstream churches and even of the politics of the President of that country. That 'God is on our side' in the shaping of the political, social and ethical agenda of a country has rarely been understood as literally as it is in today's United States.

Whatever one may think about that, it points as it were to the central importance of church history as a *grand narrative* from the development of the community of the Church to a specific contextual identity. Such a narrative presentation is by definition of fundamental importance for the community faith, as in it it gives account of its loyalty to the covenant relationship between God and human beings, between nature and supernatural order, to this covenant relationship which it regards as the foundation of its existence. Not without reason are the basic texts of the monotheistic religions, the Old and New Testaments and the Qur'an, themselves a more or less rudimentary form of the 'history of the Church; or perhaps rather of the 'history of God'. They show meanings and deliver explanations for the events and developments, the laws and values, in short for the forms, results and guidelines of the historic action (the *agency*) of the original group of believers. They do so by calibrating it with the defining intervention of God in the chances and changes of world history. This history of God indeed manifests itself as the history of the Church, since it is the Church which judges if it is a faithful representation of God's active presence.

The representation of history also takes up a central space in the self-consciousness of the churches. This applies in particular to those churches which refer – as so many Protestant communities do – to a historic moment of separation or founding as the defining moment of their credibility or which - as the Roman Catholic Church and its variations do - regard the historic development and the transfer of doctrine and moral order, that is the tradition, as a main characteristic of their authenticity. Thereby, however, they also render themselves vulnerable to the eventualities of writing history, not just through the eventualities of the ups and downs (with their bad as well as with their good aspects), but primarily through those eventualities which are connected with historiography itself as narrative strategy or analytical discourse.

Church history with or without God?

Church history has always been a form of writing the history of the church community and describing it, in which God himself plays a variety of strong, or occasionally even disappearing roles. The locus of church history is the Church, not God. He may at times be the intellectual point of reference for the group consciousness of the community of faith. He may appear as the current source of religious experience or effect the intervention of supernatural reality in the natural order. But frequently he is little more than a stopgap, the one who fills the gaps in the representation of the causes of well-being and suffering of human beings and the world. The paradox of specialization in this discipline is not so much that a history of religion without the Church might emerge but that the history of the Church frequently manages without God, without religion in the strong sense of the word.

Not just God and the Church, but even the dimension of the community of believers and their everyday lives that is not related to the Church is affected in a variety of ways by the representation of the history of the community of faith. Churches can be totally submerged in their symbiosis with society: in a political symbiosis as during the Middle Ages and the *ançien régime*, or in a cultural symbiosis such as in the national states of the nineteenth century or as in the Netherlands where in the past the life of the entire society was divided by confessional boundaries. In such contexts ecclesial values are defining for all areas of society – at least this is how the churches themselves saw it. From a non-church point of view this looked rather different, that is, the other way round: the Church takes on the norms of social development as its own values. In order to be able to form or reform society, the Church has to accommodate itself to the norms, values and customs of society – as God himself, so the theologians of old with their theology of accommodation claimed, used the world of imagination of the peoples of the Old Testament in order to be able to dictate his message with some prospect of finding understanding and success.

For the last statement one can also list endless examples. The way in which Christian churches allowed themselves to be inspired with regard to the shaping of thought, morality and ritual by the Jewish traditions, classical antiquity and the Celtic-Germanic worlds of imagination and life represents a secular development in which God plays merely a derivative role. Even the centuries of the churches' struggle against what they regarded as superstition can be read in two ways: as the brave struggle of God's faithful against the despicable influence of secular, if not satanic, powers; but also as a secular revision undertaken by the Church itself of the way in which it, or at least certain groups within it, had initially embraced the world and its magical thinking. For the definition of superstition was over the centuries subject to a rapid development. Time and time again it was readjusted in accordance with new developments in the relationship between faith and reason, in ideas about magic and the devil, of heaven and earth and the changing praxis of the world of human life. In the decades after 1970 the debate about popular piety and popular religious culture represented a new phase in the Church's laborious struggle with less desirable forms and expressions of faith and cultural practices, which the Church nevertheless has to take on board at some point with regard to its fellowship with God.

The pagan Middle Ages, as Ludo Millis called them, are a particularly significant epoch which can be read in two different ways.[2] On the one hand, one can see them as a time in which the Christian Church, in anticipation of the proactive Christianization of the Reformation and the Catholic Reform since the sixteenth century (Jean Delumeau, Keith Thomas), was still the concern of a small enlightened (genuinely Christianized) minority who lived alongside (and mentally at times even entirely separately from) the masses which still lived in paganism, its polytheistic world of imagination and its rituals of magic.[3] To write history in this way, however, means measuring history from the perspective of its most recent outcome. It is tantamount to criticizing our ancestors for not having arrived at a form of society shaped by Christian norms and values with a high level of reflection, with limited reference to religious rites and with an internalized life of faith, as has become the norm since the great Reformers and the Council of Trent. History is assessed and usually also judged from the perspective of today, from the state of thought reached at the point when the historian writes her book. When a community writes its own history, there is the genuine danger of such historical finalism, which is either characterized by self-pity or by triumphalism. The churches can escape this even less, as being institutions founded on ideals, they tend to project their ideals into the time of their origin, and subsequently use these backwards projected ideals to calibrate for their developments. This is not objectionable as such, but contemporary historians no longer regard this as a legitimate way of writing history.

This leads to two new questions: is it at all possible to write history without finalism? Can it be told without judging? These questions are as it were a function of the question behind them: is church history the most appropriate form for writing the history of the development of the relationship between God and the world? The term 'church history' can be used in two ways: literally in the sense of the history of the church community and its way of dealing with God's message in history; or in a further sense, as a master key for all forms of writing history that in some way deal with believers in the world. With regard to the latter, as a historian I prefer the term 'history of religion'; for in the historic relationship of faith and feeling between God and world, religion is in the literal sense of the word the bond between God and human beings, more universal than the contingent institutional forms which the fellowship of believers takes up. From the point of view of the churches it is, however, especially their form of organization which constitutes the community of faith. It must also be said with regard to this point of view that it is impossible for an individual to develop a meaningful understanding of God, of an encounter with God or of the relationship between the natural and supernatural order without reference to the tradition, the handing down through a community of whatever it conceives itself to have received and in whichever way it may take shape in words or become visible. In order to be recognized by the subject and to be expressed, the so-called spontaneous experience of God always requires mediation through cultural forms. However, such cultural forms develop in a group, in a community of culture and faith. And only a relationship of authority within such a group, of whichever form, is capable of making the distinction between those forms of God experience which are regarded as desirable or permissible within the respective groups and those which are not. And maybe this applies also, in accordance with the claims the churches make for themselves, to the question of their authenticity.

In this respect, 'church history' (in the literal, narrow sense of the word), as the history of the triangular relationship between God, the believer and the Church, is inevitable for those who believe in God and his Church. Church history has always focused on three aspects, that is, the community of believers itself, on God, a relational entity independent of context (of whichever kind of transcendence), and on the world outside of the realm of faith, that is, the context in which the community of faith can make itself manifest. Different types of relationship to history emerge depending on the desires and needs of the community of faith and on its attitude to the other two focuses. Believers and believing historians in particular are required at some point to be able to make a judgement about the rightness of the way that their community has gone through history, that is, about its relationship to history. Those who reject such a judgement condemn historiography to be a clinical form of documentation without clout in society.

For regardless of the question whether we have to judge, we inevitably do judge. Even historians who are not themselves involved in the Church, or historians who have left their involvement in the Church behind when they took up their subject, make judgements. Anticlerical historiography has probably done even greater damage in the field than that influenced by clericalism. But the criteria by which such outsiders judge are different. They are not those of the holistic perspective on the whole, which is being formed by the Church and theology and where the criteria of assessment refer to the object of judgement itself. They are rather criteria which first and foremost are borrowed from the practice of their subject, their scholarly discipline. This does not necessarily render a greater or lesser truth with regard to the representation of history, but rather a different form of validity and power of expression, that is, one which puts God in his role as *actor* or co-actors in brackets, and which looks for the validity of historical representation exclusively in the categories of the representation of human activity and faith. The history of the success of the evangelization of unbelieving nations, to name but one example, can at the same time become a report of the catastrophes of the destruction of indigenous norms, values and patterns of behaviour, which on the assumption that something can be understood better from within could have achieved just as much if not more for the proclamation of the Christian message. This applies to the account of the Chinese ritual controversy or (*mutatis mutandis*) to the presentation of the Jesuit Reductions in Paraguay. There, fundamental community institutions which we would nowadays regard as the domain of cultural anthropology were ultimately destroyed by missionaries, as the church community as such was obviously not capable of perceiving itself as an entity outside of the world of western culture, imagery, symbolism and behaviour.

The craft of the historian and interdisciplinary work

Here too we have to make a distinction between two developments: from of old there have been objectivizing forms of historiography about religion, the Church and faith which borrow their methods from the tools of the historian and which do indeed remain inside the discipline of history as it has developed during the last three to four centuries. But there is also a form of writing history which transcends the boundaries of its discipline. From the awareness that faith, religion and the Church are phenomena which are broadly rooted in society, it looks for help for its historical analysis and does so from other disciplines such as psychology and psychiatry, sociology and cultural anthropology, linguistics and communication studies. In addition, this is the only way in which historiography is able to cope with two apparent anomalies which can nowadays be observed in the world of religion and faith: religion without the Church and without Christian faith, mere ritual, but as such rich and full of meaning; and on the other hand forms of belief without the visible formation of communities and ritual and without the discipline of the Church.

The first development, historiography as a craft, began as it were very early on with the emergence and the early growth of church history as a subject in which the community of faith systematically gives itself an account of its past and its legitimacy. To this end they developed rudimentary methods of selection, reduction or even glorification of historical events and life stories, of apologetics aimed at those outside (heathen and heretics) and the direction of the faith community's collective consciousness. Literary genres such as the *passio*, the account of the suffering of martyrs, and of the *vita*, the lives of saints, which continue to exist today, are such methods of writing history which we are now seeking to analyse critically using methods of literary criticism and psychology. Eusebius of Caesarea, Gregory of Tours, the Venerable Bede and others during the first millennium developed models of ecclesial historiography which for us have taken on the whiff of church history as we know it. In their own day and age, however, their perspectives and methods were major movements of renewal in the writing of church history. The schisms of the sixteenth century in turn also introduced methodological innovations, as the arguments of apostolic continuity, or of breaking with the unfortunate past legitimized the separation and thereby granted church history a lead role in the area of theological studies.

The twelve parts of the *Annales ecclesiastici* of Caesar Baronius were so influential for the relationships between the churches that the Dutch Provincial State undertook to set up a special chair at the Protestant University of Leiden dedicated to combating the historical view of this work. It was occupied by one of the greatest scholars of his day, Claude Saumaise, who was headhunted from France and paid a substantial salary for it. Saumaise was no longer a member of the theology faculty but outranked it. His philological historical methods, which regarded even the dogmas themselves as the result of historical developments, were the beginning of historiography as a discipline in its own right. This rapidly led to the development of archaeology, which was no longer within a theological paradigm but used the starting points and methods of philosophy and then of the humanities and of cultural studies.

On the Catholic side, they found their counterpart in the Bollandists' *Acta Sanctorum*, an endless sober string of editions of saints' lives. These were on balance treated like secular sources to which philosophical methods were applied, while the scholars, largely Jesuit in origin, were not too bothered about divine inspiration. This is the moment when we can begin to speak of a fragmentation of church history as a theological discipline. Church history could still be used as an argument in theological debates, but its own method of argumentation no longer corresponded to the internal logic of theology.

It is certainly not true to say that church history went downhill from there. On the contrary: by making use of what it could gain from autonomous historical methods, its internal powers of persuasion increased, even if it probably played a lesser role than it had in the previous four centuries when it came to the social location of the churches with regard to their identity. However, since then a second form of specialization has taken place which heightened the sense of fragmentation. This is the emerging interdisciplinary work in the humanities. This is based on the gradual but accelerating loss of the conviction that there is a hierarchy of disciplines with regard to their content, in which some are subordinate to others and the discipline at the top can and must determine the development of those disciplines beneath it. Initially, this primary discipline was theology. As such it was able to demand that history, especially that of the Church, had to be done in line with its own aims and its own developments. The development towards an equality of the disciplines tore down such presumptuous claims and at the same time enabled the differentiation of the object proper to church history. The compulsive fixation on the Church as an institution, on the teaching of the Church and on the norms of the Church, on clergy and theology, was disrupted and room was created for the individual and for dissent, for community and gender, that is, socially constructed gender roles, for sacrality outside the norm and for rituals without Christian faith.

History of the Church or history of religion?

Then there is no more reason to be afraid of the flowering of the history of religion, of the history of faith and the Church outside of traditional church history. The problem is not in the method or in interdisciplinarity. Some kind of non-theological approach has been used in the writing of history about the churches for centuries. Or rather, church historians have never been afraid to use the tools of their trade as historians. The same applies to interdisciplinary working. Since the Middle Ages philosophy (as the *ancilla theologiae*), philology and other alpha disciplines were part of the theologians' basic tool kit and thus also of the historians among them. This interdisciplinary work is rarely noticed, but it is not that different from the way in which historians today refer to social sciences such as cultural anthropology or medical disciplines such as psychiatry. In the eyes of non-theological disciplines, faith, religious practice, church communities and all other forms of individual and corporate realization of the desire for God or of encounters with God are social practices to which the rules of their discipline must be applied without restriction. Contrasts such as between secular and theological or sacred scholarship are of no importance here. 'Secular' religious science from which God is 'excluded' is no less capable of analysing religious ritual, mystical symbolism or theological thought. On the contrary, other disciplines lay bare before the eyes of theology those dimensions which are hidden. They show how human action, human ideas and human thinking, even with regard to religion, can be connected, even must be connected, with the entire broad area of studying human beings as active, artistic and thinking subjects. The holistic desire of theology in the light of the double fragmentation outlined above therefore does not disappear altogether but gains another area of work. What has changed greatly is the object of its scholarly approach. This is turned by 45 degrees, from the vertical to the horizontal direction: religion as fundamental human practice, the world of human imagination, human ideas.

Thus we now have to come back to church history. Church history has internal aims and external aims. Internally, it is concerned with group cohesion and acknowledging a group's right to exist. As such church history is closely connected with the theological paradigm. More importantly, from of old church history is the most appropriate means for a group to create identity, for human beings, even human beings of faith, are essentially beings who exist in time and within a group (and are thus social beings). In this position church historians always ask the questions by which their scholarly effort is guided: where do we come from and where are we going? This puts a specific burden on all discussions about church historians and historians of other disciplines or with the uninitiated. Even before outsiders become aware of it, they begin to tread on the psychological toes of the group. And even before the group becomes aware of it, it is in danger of assuming a finalist understanding of itself which is in contrast to science – not merely to the science of western rationality, but also to the science of other cultures and continents which are shaped by different kinds of rationality. It is one of the characteristics of science to be able to step outside of one's own logic and to allow for a broader rationality, whether generalizing or narrative, which guides thought and action or offers a rational explanation of it.

But is this what church history as a theological discipline wants to achieve? How far does church history want to go in its obligation towards the straitjacket of scientific rules? Does it want to create a niche for itself where a different set of rules apply? From the outside, the main problem for church history is that in the past it took the point of view of the Church or at least church-directed and authorized theology or made it the object of its study. It was a form of historiography which relied on the church institution, its values and its discipline, and which reinterpreted the faith experience of individuals from a corporate perspective instead of seeing them as in themselves formative for the community. Believers who thought of themselves as individuals who did not want to be put under the yoke of ecclesial structures were 'chrétiens sans Église' (L. Kolakowski) or, even more strongly expressed, 'stepchildren of Christianity' (J. Lindeboom).

Even more than the social sciences, the emergence of cultural history is a threat for the conventional practice of church history. Sociology of religion never questioned the church institution as the central starting point of history, while cultural history calls it into question, as culture is being passed on collectively but nevertheless allows for individual experience, thinking and lifestyle and even legitimizes them. Cultural history is less concerned with structures than with *agency*, with activity. Thus the institutional influence of church history becomes the subject of critical discussion. Not that this is insignificant, but it can no longer be taken for granted as our historical perspective on religion. The Church, according to cultural historians, is constituted in the interaction between supply and demand, between human beings who want to shape this faith and institutions which want to support them in doing so. Thus it is no longer clear whose the initiative is here and who in the end determines the result. I therefore plead for more of a church history from below, from the perspective of the faithful, that is, from the point of view of 'demand'. This I prefer to call 'history of religion', for this is about the *religio*, understood as the living, connecting bond with God, not as an abstract religious system.[4] Therefore it can only be a history of being affected and not a mere bloodless science of religion. For does theology primarily always have to be concerned with the faithful themselves and then with the Church, the community of faith, about ecclesiology and the relevant institutional church history? A church history without the object God is nothing new. Neither is a church history for which God is no longer the source of inspiration. But a 'church history' (or whatever we want to call it) which has God as its object and source of inspiration has added value, not for the subject of historiography as such but for those concerned. And yet, from the point of view of the historian, I dare say that a history of religion, of faith and of the Church (in this order) is infinitely preferable, that is, as a broad cross link between the disciplines, from theology to the humanities to the behavioural sciences. For none of them has a monopoly on the believer/the human being of faith.

Translated by Natalie K. Watson based on the German translation by Ansgar Ahlbrecht.

Notes

1. Donald B. Kraybill and Carl Desportes Bowman, 2001, *On the Backroad to Heaven: Old Order Hutterites, Mennonites, Amish, and Brethren*, Baltimore and London: Center Books in Anabaptist Studies.
2. Ludo Millis (ed.), 1991, *De Heidense Middeleuwen*, Brussels and Rome.
3. Jean Delumeau, 1977, *Catholicism between Luther and Voltaire: A New View of the Counter-Reformation*, trans. Jeremy Moiser, London; Keith Thomas, 1971, *Religion and the Decline of Magic: Studies in Popular Beliefs in Sixteenth and Seventeenth-Century England*, London.
4. Cf. Willem Frijhoff, 2002, *Embodied Belief: Ten Essays on Religious Culture in Dutch History*, Studies in Religious History, ReLic: Hilversum.

III. Fragmentation and Specialization: Attempts to Reconnect

From Shaken Foundations to a Different Integrity: Spirituality as Response to Fragmentation

MARY GREY

Little did Paul Tillich realize when he titled his sermons in 1946 *The Shaking of the Foundations* that the following fifty years would witness increasingly to the haunting experience that 'the centre does not hold', that great pillars of certainty would tumble with the loss of great meta-narratives, and that Christian faith would teeter confusedly between two poles: whether to withstand attempts to impose new universalisms or lapse into competing relativisms.[1] For many believing Christians the choice seemed stark: hang onto the old certainties and the conviction that truth is a seamless web, or relapse into competing versions of truth, conflicting historical analyses and contextual struggles for justice. This invitation to relativism has brought cynicism and despair to many. But to others it stimulated a new spiritual quest, a genuine attempt to create a life where an integrated whole and harmonious ordering would restore meaning. Many see this as the background to the resurgence of spirituality, blossoming throughout all religions and even beyond religious circles. This article attempts to discern how successful these spiritualities are in constituting a Christian response to the fragmentation of culture.

Spirituality – what could it be?

The word 'spirituality' is certainly a neologism – beginning to flourish comparatively recently from the French *spiritualité*, since the *Dictionnaire de Spiritualité, ascétique et mystique* began to appear in 1932.[2] To appreciate the speed of recent developments and their popularity it is only necessary to compare *The Study of Spirituality* of Cheslyn Jones and his colleagues (1986) with the new *SCM Dictionary of Spirituality* (2005) edited by Philip Sheldrake, to see the new areas that spirituality now embraces.[3] Whereas the focus on the Bible, mysticism and the spirituality of religious congregations is retained and deepened, far more attention is now given to the body, sexuality, nature, justice and indigenous spiritualities.

It is not only the word 'spirituality', but the concept of spiritual experience itself that would not have been easily recognized by the early Christians: for these, faith in Jesus Christ was expressed by coming together to break bread, by concern for the needy, and by preaching the gospel as the Lord had commanded. Later, the Orthodox Church would recognize spiritual experience not as belonging to an individual, but as the liturgical reality of the gathered community in the Sunday Eucharist. This is light years away from the contemporary idea of a spirituality expressing the search for an all-encompassing wholeness, in which to integrate the experience of self, world and God. And to integrate this as *lived practice*, not as theory alone.

Spirituality began tentatively to approach the modern definition when new contexts demanded diverse expressions of faith. For example, when monks first retreated into the deserts of Egypt and Palestine from the third century onwards, their lives were characterized by a chosen asceticism, in protest against the extravagance and corruption of contemporary culture.[4] This sense of discerning what dimensions of faith should be highlighted as leitmotivs, giving meaning to the whole spiritual life, came to be the inspiration for the development of the idea of spirituality. In the growth of the monastic congregations, from the Benedictines onwards, it is remarkable to see the diversity of the chosen charisms, be they the balance of prayer and work (Benedictine), poverty and simplicity (Franciscan), to the contemporary focus on reconciliation of, for example, the Taizé community in France and Sant'Egidio in Italy. (Of course it is necessary to understand the charisms in the broader religious, historical and cultural context of the times to which they are a response.)

Spirituality – the contemporary focus

Amid the fragmented state of contemporary culture, it is indisputable that individualism flourishes in a society where the ethos of the market – a profit-driven consumerism – has established reign. Inevitably market-inspired language has crept into spirituality. Harvey Cox describes how the discourse of the Market (or Mammon) is comparable in scope – if not profundity – to the *Summa* of Aquinas, or the works of Karl Barth.[5] At the apex of the system, of course, is the market as god, a market with divine attributes, we are assured, even if not visible to us. But this is a new phenomenon:

From Shaken Foundations to a Different Integrity

Since the earliest stages of human history there have been bazaars, rialtos, and trading posts – all markets. But the market was never God, because there were other centres of value and meaning, other gods. Only in the past two centuries has the Market risen above these demigods and chthonic spirits to become today's First Cause.[6]

With its own liturgies, sacraments, priests and seers of its mysteries the market penetrates the domain of spirituality itself. Cox remarks:

> previously unmarketable states of grace as serenity are now appearing in its catalogues, what was once only to be acquired through ascetic disciplines like prayer and fasting are now commodified through aromatherapy or 'a weekend workshop in a Caribbean resort with a sensitive psychological consultant replacing the crotchety retreat master'.[7]

New Age

Within this social context three contemporary currents of spirituality are selected, each depicting how spirituality attempts to create a wholeness amid cultural confusion. The first is, unsurprisingly, the eclectic mix that calls itself 'New Age'. New Age spirituality – almost by definition indefinable! – can be seen as symbolic of cultural fragmentation, as rejection of traditional religious structures that stifle the spirit, yet itself not innocent of market seductions, as the above quotations show. Many aspects of New Age, like Goddess religions and Nature religions, do manifest a sincere struggle for wholeness and coherence, seeing patriarchy as destructive of the earth and femaleness alike; but others, in their attempts to achieve wholeness, in their rejection of what they construe as authoritarian and dominating dimensions of tradition, fall into another form of fragmentation in their arbitrary choice of certain attractive elements of spirituality but the exclusion of others. For example, meditation without the necessary discipline, reading Tarot cards, peering at crystals, may coexist with the music of Abbess Hildegard of Bingen, with no recognition – or reclaiming – of the theological content and monastic discipline that framed her life. Gregorian chant tops the charts regularly, but the goal sought by its devotees is more likely to be a transient sense of transcendental harmony bearing no relation to Benedictine spirituality. Buddhist meditation before breakfast is popular with certain groups of business people. But there is no evidence that this practice acts as benchmark for the ethical principles acted on during the economic discussions that follow.

None of these forms of spirituality may be intrinsically harmful, but, sadly, while situated within the fragmentation of culture, they may feed the very individualism and self-indulgence from which their adherents wish to distance themselves.

Reclaim the past

This may also be true of the second current of spirituality: this is the process of reclaiming the past, but within a certain unhistorical and idealized glow. A good example of this is Celtic spirituality, now widely known throughout Europe – and even America.[8] Focusing on the Christian saints of the Celtic Church in Wales, Ireland, Scotland, north-east England and Cornwall, as well as Brittany and parts of Germany, many Christians discover here a form of community that is more loosely structured, often opposed to the authoritarian government of the Roman Church, and more concerned, they imagine, with love of creation than with sin and guilt.[9] The relationship of the saints to nature, trees, birds and animals is inspiring and leads to a sense of the sacramentality of the whole of creation. Wholeness is experienced within the sense that the entirety of life is blessed, even the humblest of activities. The problem here – without wanting to reject any element that leads to deepening of faith – is again that certain elements are selected and others ignored. The presumption that gender relations were more egalitarian in Celtic times cannot be historically proved. There are deeply dualistic and sin-centred elements in Celtic theology, which, in any case, cannot be lumped into one category. Its reality is more diverse and complex. Gilbert Markus and Thomas Clancy point out that the lyrical poems, supposedly of Celtic hermits living in harmony with nature, are more likely to have been written later as a form of escapism for scholarly monks:

> For them it is an alternative to the routine concerns and frustrations of life in a noisy and busy monastery. A real hermit, living in a damp stone or wooden cell, fasting in hot and cold weather to subdue the flesh, terrified of thunder and lightning . . . is not the author of these 'nature poems'.[10]

This is not to deny that certain elements remain inspirational: Ian Bradley, while debunking a simplistic, unhistorical approach, still admits that friendship with birds and animals is a remarkable feature of Celtic spirituality – although not confined to this period alone.[11]

A mystical-prophetic spirituality for a fragmented culture

How then can spirituality address fragmentation without imposing false universalism, or obliterating difference and complexity? The most urgent task is to address the 'I' of the self who seeks wholeness. As long as the self is locked within the market ethos discussed above, there is no escape from self-indulgent, narcissistic consumerism. Unsurprisingly, much attention in contemporary spirituality is focused on the *practice* of revisioning the self. Thus feminist and ecological spiritualities stress the fact of the *embodied* self, embodied in a historical context and in an environment that is either nurturing, enabling healthy development, or preventing this, through physical or emotional deprivation. The self is *gendered*, so attention is focused on socio-cultural barriers to the full becoming of both women and men and the structural barriers that block it, such as the prejudices and laws that are part and parcel of patriarchal societies. Recognition of the '*ecological* self', dependent on earth, water, air and agriculture, now leads to a sense of interdependence between the human and non-human, where 'care' is re-visioned to include care for the earth and a sense of reverence for place. The self develops in connection not only with the earth but in relationship to interlocking *communities* of family, friends, faith community and country. So spiritual practice, in dying to the self of narcissism, is widened to include perspectives of care and justice within these circles of community. Finally, the self is always in process, always in pilgrimage, always dying to the former moment and moving to another self-moment, as ageing, life experiences, events and commitments call for new responses. The death of a child, the experience of chronic pain and life-threatening sickness, the wounds of violence and poverty, all call forth the self into new self-moments, like the chrysalis shedding a skin. The connected self within a spiritual journey is always called to make new connections, yet never to lose touch with the wisdom of past experience. But the self-moment that is left behind (the carefree child, the adventurous adolescent, the rapturous lover, the freedom fighter, the lonely widow) is not left behind as fragment, but as self-moment that will in the fullness of time, through power and presence of God, be gathered into the wholeness of full personhood. This is the process we call spirituality.

It is prophetic, first, in the counter-culture and practice it inspires, in this case counter to the ethos of the market. If the market's success depends on feeding insatiable desires for material goods, Christian spirituality turns this on its head, revealing it as a degrading view of humanity, and relocating desire as longing for God.¹² God is experienced as both the source of our passion for justice – for right relation between humanity and creation – as Wisdom (Sophia), teaching us how to reclaim the past, and as nurturing presence, inspiring a different ethics and practice. God's love is experienced as embodied love of creation, as love prioritizing the poorest and most vulnerable of people and creatures. Within prophetic spirituality, the peoples suffering most from the oppressive economic systems find voice: enabling their flourishing in an effective solidarity builds bridges across fragmented cultures.

Second, this is also a *mystical* spirituality. It was Karl Rahner who said that if there was to be a Christianity, a Christian would be a mystic or nothing at all.[13] The primary meaning of mysticism is the contemplation of the mysteries, the mysteries of God – and that is the heart of the liturgy.[14] But liturgy is expressive of a wider reality: sacramentality is the graced experience of the whole of life, even amid pain and violence. The aim of a mystical relation with God is the restoration of wholeness, or union, in the midst of fragmentation and brokenness, a situation sometimes called the Dark Night. What would it mean to reclaim mysticism, not as the private experience of an individual, indeed not primarily as 'experience' as such, but as the spiritual journey of the community? If that sounds like a democratization of mysticism, a focus on immanence instead of transcendence, a focus on embodiedness, on connectedness with this earth rather than flight from it, there is still something here that challenges the fragmentation and individualism of culture that could truly be called the 'Dark Night'. I wrote earlier:

> The Dark Night comprehends a much deeper level of alienation and despair. It is a darkness born of lack of nourishment in the liturgy, prayer life and doctrine . . . It is the pain of distorted symbols and lifeless rituals. . . . : it is the making of the Christ mystery into something unrelated to human living and the controlling of this by a clerical elite . . . it is having no form of prayer that connected with one's life experience, having the life of the spirit choked back and still-born . . . The total impasse of the night, the experience of being made mute and inarticulate – not in the silence of loving contemplation, but because the language sought for has not yet been brought to birth – descends with shocking immediacy.[15]

The darkness referred to here is that of being blocked, being starved of true nourishment, the situation of many today in a fragmented culture. And

From Shaken Foundations to a Different Integrity   85

yet, the dark night can usher in new dawns, can function as epiphany of something not yet experienced. In that ambiguity and tension of the mystical Dark Night, dark spirals deeper. Mysticism as community response in faith can be experienced through the 'transfiguration' of existence, through I-and-Thou relationships of mutuality and through political action for justice, as the late Dorothee Sölle knew so well.[16] In radical protest for peace, in leaving comfort zones to resist the evil of dominating systems, this, for Sölle and her activist groups, was the place of revelation of the mysteries of God.

To enter into the experience of transfigured existence sounds perhaps like something only for poets. But too long has the aesthetic been neglected by theology. The intuition is that this is offered to all as a permeation of sacred power through our ordinary lives, as potential for wholeness. It follows from a recognition and deep appreciation that all creation is theophanic, revelatory of the Divine. This shines out of Orthodox theology, from much of Celtic theology, ecofeminist and liberation spiritualities. For example, Bishop Kallistos of the Greek Orthodox Church cites a lyrical passage about a tree, critically noting that the poet does not take the further step of acknowledging the creator.[17] The transfigured tree for Kallistos means Creation is 'theophanic... The world is Sacrament'. The world is *iconic*. He relates: Father Amphilochius (d. 1970), an 'elder' on the island of Patmos, used to say, 'God gave another commandment not recorded in Scripture: "Love the Trees... when you plant trees, you plant hope, you plant peace, you plant love, and you will receive God's blessing."' But many mystical descriptions of trees, for Kallistos, miss the point – that it is the tree as mediating God's presence which is the essential element. Thus Moses, in the encounter with the burning Bush: 'In and through the tree he beholds, Moses enters into communion with the living God.'

Then comes an ethical command – take off your shoes (dead and lifeless objects). He is standing on holy ground because the earth – the entire created reality – is sacred. This is a way of seeing, perceiving, tasting, listening, experiencing the entire world as permeated by the presence and graciousness of God. The mystical quality is in the quality of perception, but also in the lasting nature of the visionary element. This is how novelist Annie Dillard spoke of the lasting quality of the vision of the 'Tree with Lights' in it:

> I saw the backyard cedar where the mourning doves roost charged and transfigured, each cell buzzing with flame. I stood on the grass with the

lights in it, grass that was wholly fire, utterly focused and utterly dreamed. It was less like seeing than like being for the first time seen, knocked breathless by a powerful glance. The flood of fire abated, but I'm still spending the power . . . The vision comes and goes, mostly goes, but I live for it, for the moment when the mountains open and a new light roars in spate through the crack, and the mountains slam.[18]

The vision of the tree with lights in it is not a private vision reserved for the privileged but an invitation to perceptive witness of creation as community commitment. It arose because of the patient attention Annie Dillard had given to life on Tinker Creek. 'Listening with empathy', 'patient attention', 'steadfastly searching', 'remembering', 'respecting practical wisdom' and resistance to injustice are the modes of this spirituality looking for wholeness.

A new integrity?

But this is not the end of the story. Seamless unity is no longer a goal. The last century's resistance to false universalism and openness to diversity has at least taught us this. The spiritual journey takes place in a sinful, conflictual world. We as spiritual searchers are flawed human beings, fragmentation deeply etched in our psyches. Maybe the gospel story gives a clue as to the shape of the new integrity. When those five thousand people on the mountain had been fed, the fragments filled twelve baskets. This new collection was not a perfect loaf: 'they took up twelve baskets full of the broken pieces left over', wrote Matthew (14.20). Thus our flawed, fragmented selves must learn to struggle with diversity, doubt, ambiguity and conflicting accounts of truth, always refusing simplistic solutions. Only then do we admit the possibility that flawed crystals may become 'immortal diamonds', as the poet Gerard Manley Hopkins expressed it.[19]

Spirituality then becomes the process of 'gathering the fragments': through privileging insights from vulnerable and marginalized communities, through facing the challenge of the Dark Night of unknowing and the possibility of failure, flawed crystals become reshaped into a new, more modest and humble integrity or wholeness. Here the courage not to renege on the search and to follow the Divine Spirit into uncharted territory are crucial way markers for Christian witness and spiritual journeying.

Notes

1. Paul Tillich, 1949, *The Shaking of the Foundations*, London: SCM Press. The phrase 'the Centre does not hold' is from W. B. Yeats, 1991, 'The Second Coming', in *Selected Poetry*, London: Penguin, p. 124.
2. Joseph de Guibert et al., 1932, Paris.
3. Cheslyn Jones, Geoffrey Wainwright, Edward Yarnold (eds), 1986, *The Study of Spirituality*, London: SPCK; Philip Sheldrake (ed.), 2005, *The New SCM Dictionary of Spirituality*, London: SCM Press.
4. See Jones et al., *The Study of Spirituality*, Part 11, 'The Early Fathers', pp. 102–18.
5. Harvey Cox, 1999, 'The Market as God: Living in the New Dispensation', *The Atlantic* 283:3.
6. Cox, 'The Market as God', p. 3.
7. Cox, 'The Market as God', p. 8.
8. Another example would be an idealized, unhistorical reclaiming of St Francis.
9. A good example of this is the Synod of Whitby in CE 664 called by the abbess Hilda of Whitby. Here the Celtic Church opposed the Roman Church – led by St Wilfrid – over the date of Easter, celebrated according to different calendars by each. Needless to say, Rome won.
10. T. Clancy and G. Markus, 1995, *Iona: The Earliest Poetry of a Celtic Monastery*, Edinburgh: Edinburgh University Press, p. 90.
11. Ian Bradley, 1998, 'How Green was Celtic Christianity?', *Ecotheology* 4, pp. 58–69.
12. See Mary Grey, 2003, *Sacred Longings: An Ecofeminist Theology and Globalization*, London: SCM Press.
13. Karl Rahner, 1966, 'Frömmigkeit früher und heute', in *Schriften zur Theologie*, vol. VII, Einsiedeln, Zürich, Köln: Herder, pp. 11–31: 'Der Fromme von Morgen wird ein "Mystiker" sein, einer, der etwas "erfahren" hat, oder er wird nicht mehr sein . . .', p. 22.
14. This was the original meaning of spiritual experience, as I mentioned earlier.
15. Mary Grey, 1979, *Redeeming the Dream*, London: SPCK, pp. 75–7.
16. See Dorothee Sölle, 2001, *The Silent Cry: Mysticism and Resistance*, Augsburg Fortress Press.
17. See Bishop Kallistos, 1997, 'From Creation to the Creator', *Ecotheology* 2, pp. 8–30, quotation p. 11.
18. Annie Dillard, 1982, *Pilgrim at Tinker Creek*, London: Bantam Books, pp. 33–4.
19. Gerard Manley Hopkins, 1953, 'That Nature is a Heraclitean Fire and of the Glory of the Resurrection', in *Poems and Prose*, London: Penguin, pp. 65–6.

Theologies of the South: Incarnate and Holistic

DIEGO IRARRAZABAL

When it speaks of God, each community does so from its immersion in a historical process; its speech has particular characteristics from which it makes contact with other subjects. In the developed world, discourses on God have used philosophy and interacted with secular sciences, and their prolific specialization has been sanctioned by modern reasoning. In the developing world (which makes up two-thirds of the total), reflection is more attuned to a whole range of sciences and spiritualities, and Christianity tends to be thought of in terms of service to a new humanity. Nevertheless, our theological institutions generally reproduce and adapt models worked out in the West.

This has been changing. During the last forty years various forms of 'thinking the faith'[1] have sprung up and developed, contextual, liberating and 'other-worldly' (in the sense that 'a different world is possible').[2] How do we relate to North Atlantic achievements? It is better to interact with them, rather than remain subject to them, since interaction between them and us strengthens capacities for reflecting on and celebrating faith both here and there.

I propose to look at the global scenario and the existence of various discourses. I shall point to theologies of particular and universal subjects, and I shall stress the wisdom of the believing people. Do such specialized forms of knowledge help us to understand the whole of reality in the light of faith? How do individual contributions fit into the project of universal happiness? To the eyes of faith, the specific and universal calling to happiness is inspired by the Spirit of God.

Globalization and partial discourses

Theological discourse tends to approach the human condition in the singular, and it thereby presupposes an abstract subject and a developed-world background. We are invited to succumb to western paradigms that include many modern values but shrink from complexity, exploit nature, reify the human body, and employ the subject–object duality.³ When theological discourse is bipolar, soul and body are opposed, doctrine is simplified into saving oneself from sin, and God is seen as an object of study. This dualist conceptualization is remote from the gospel and can become idolatrous in character.

The emergent theologies are very different, giving pride of place to the incarnation and Easter, with their bodily and historical dimensions. With regard to God, the theologies of the South stress the relational aspect. So there is no human subject who can own the truth and give voice to universality; there are rather different believing faces that speak from 'other' modernities in favour of small hopes that become universal. In Brazil, Maria da Soledade has noted that 'liberation theology has been a light . . . by which I have discovered little signs of the Kingdom, beautiful things hidden in society's trash', and she adds the thought of an illiterate friend: 'as I cannot live without the air I breathe, so I cannot live without God in my life'.⁴ These symbolic ways of understanding faith go beyond unvarying and unhistorical concepts. By the light of faith, the community understands human events with their lights and shadows. At the end of the day, believing discourse is not something 'about' a god-object but a matter of being 'with' the Living God.

The theologies of the South spring from the periphery of society and are radical both in their confrontation with hegemonic paradigms and in their belief in liberation from sin. We face up to the planetary hegemony, we observe its crossovers and minglings, and we deduce alternative courses. Using sensible socio-cultural and philosophical approaches, we not only lament oppression and meaninglessness; we also value the economic and political resources to be found in marginalized peoples, not to mention so many sources of wisdom in both women and men. Thanks to these contributions by those who are both poor and wise, events in the world can be read in different lights. These readings unite realist critique with the production of alternatives. Such readings cannot be sacralized, since every human action is challenged and reconstructed by the Word of salvation.

The question of the poor is a complex one. The poor are dehumanized by their lack of coherence and solidarity, as well as by an unjust world system. But the poor are also subjects who assimilate and reorientate modern achievements (even though these are one-sided and discriminatory). In particular they assimilate and reconstruct science and technology; there is also a crossing of boundaries thanks to communications media, together with critical and constructive reasoning, an enjoyment of material progress, and a rediscovery of harmony with the environment and democratic collaboration. In the final analysis, when marginalized people develop their own economic, cultural and spiritual resources, they de-absolutize progress, and they face up to the modern polytheism surrounding objects and individuals. The emergent theologies are challenging to today's idols, and they adhere to the one God of Life.

The believing people, and those who walk with them with theological dedication, are challenged by the gospel. Its message is cutting: 'Why do you not know how to interpret the present time?' (Luke 12.56). This uncertainty leads one to seek signs of the Kingdom in initiatives from peoples that have been left behind, and in their ways of re-creating modernity. First among these are signs of cross-fertilization between the local and the global (sometimes called *glocalization*), such as the informal commercial networks that function outside the rules of the world market. Local linked to global also accounts for 'mixed-race' Christianities (which oppose the 'western Christian' monoculture). We should not forget that 'people will come from east and west, from north and south, and will eat in the kingdom of God' (Luke 13.29). Thanks to the good news of the Kingdom, our theological currents have inter-religious features: reflection on the Christian faith does not disqualify religions other than one's own, since they are no obstacle to salvation.

The emergent theologies spy out a change of epoch, and they do so from partial and mixed-race modernities, as well as from their limited and specific hopes. That is, daily life and life as a whole both provide human alternatives; the faith reflection emerging in the developing world dialogues with these and is nourished by them. This reflection in turn is challenged by economic initiatives of the poor in solidarity who refuse to give in to privatization. It also provides resistance to the promotion that seeks to 'North-Atlanticize' our dreams (Chile is a particular example of wanting to be like the United States). In positive terms, we are challenged by local and inculturated experiences of the sacred, and by many small-scale initiatives that feed into one another. In this humble and realistic fashion we digest global challenges and propositions. This cannot be caricatured as anti-globalization, since what we have is something positive: we are *for* a different world.

With regard to partial discourses, we need to draw some distinctions. In today's world the predominant culture is that of pragmatic and specialized knowledge, the partial nature of which serves as a function of the market in cultural goods and services. Elsewhere, the actual plans and wisdoms of the ordinary people give them a discourse that is scientific and holistic in character. In the South, while some modes of Christian reflection adopt the first type of partiality, other 'partial' discourses also exist, derived from the sufferings and the positive steps taken by the ordinary people.

These local discourses opt holistically for life. This is most clearly seen in the heterogeneous world of festivals and rituals, with their symbolic potentiality and their special logic of joy in the midst of need.[5] I believe that the festive discourse of the people carries with it an incarnate and paschal theology. One can also weigh the wisdom at work in networks of human rights, in the fairness that respects gender differences, in so much relief work aimed at providing holistic health, an economy that works for all, an ecology starting from the poor, reflection on a better world. These effective discourses emanating from ordinary and poor sectors of the population have greater consistency than the postmodern language of elites that over-emphasize what differentiates and fragments for its own sake. Furthermore, appreciating the small stories that emerge from the people does not imply adherence to the relativism that rejects historical changes and sets aside the truth that makes us free.

Emerging theologies

As do all theologies, those of the South also see how salvation in Christ affects humankind and creation. So why do we assign adjectives such as 'of the South', 'contextual' or 'liberation', when we are all reflecting on the faith? Such terms point to particular aspects and methods through which the universal love of God is understood. For several centuries Christian theology has been anchored in North Atlantic concepts, which have become the norm in modern thought. Since the second half of the twentieth century, theologies have been emerging from the South. These also use the same thought processes but subordinate them (to a greater or lesser degree) to wisdoms that express their own and that re-create conditions in the contemporary world. In this way, when they reflect on salvation in Christ, the communities of the South develop their own hermeneutics.

The new theologies admire and praise the mystery of God, which has definitely saved humankind and creation. This has been expressed since the first Congress of the Association of Third-World Theologians (EATWOT), held in Tanzania in 1976.[6] It spoke of voices from Africa, Asia and America: 'men and women ... with the cultural and religious trappings of the peoples of the three continents . . . we affirm our faith in Christ, whom we praise with joy'. The Tanzania document expresses regret that 'the theologies of Europe and North America are dominant in our churches', and postulates 'interpreting the Word of God in relation to our own reality'. It also states that the religions and cultures of the Third World 'have a place in God's universal plan and that the Spirit of God is working in them'. Since this Third-World current has been misinterpreted on account of its stress on social change and as an ethic rather than a proper theology, it is worth emphasizing that from the outset it has embraced the requirements of faith, has been alive to cultures and spiritualities, and has taken account of the overall pattern of revelation of God's love.

I should like (with due acknowledgement) to devote a few lines to the lucid and prophetic theological work being done in Asia. There they are reflecting in the midst of social injustice and the impoverishment of millions, of religious pluralism, of movements for a full humanity, of the resurgence of women, of harmony with creation. This is the summary made by M. Amaladoss, for whom 'living in freedom' is a symbol shared by different Christian, Hindu, Buddhist, Islamic and cosmic traditions.

Where science and technology are concerned, Amaladoss sees the problems not so much in them as such but in the way they are used to discriminate against other ways of living. As for human and spiritual values held in common, these derive not from some 'natural law . . . or from an abstract rational philosophy' but rather from dialogue and 'dynamic consensus with no full stop'.[7] Specific interaction among people from different traditions who are on the side of life is therefore proposed. Through this pluralist attitude, theological discourse is learning to recognize the presence of God, of the Word and of his Spirit in different cultures and religions. Reciprocity with other forms of belief enriches properly Christian understanding of salvation.

I shall also comment briefly on reflections made in various groups and 'life projects' in Africa.[8] These take account of traditional religions (which still influence adherents of both Christianity and Islam), as well as of the rise and spread of independent churches with their emphasis on the Spirit. K. Bediaco has shown that, thanks to Africa, Christianity moved during the twentieth century to being a mainly non-western religion, and he adds that in African theology the faith of ordinary people carries greater weight. Besides divergent beliefs and thought-processes, there are lines of convergence, such as beliefs in the life force, rituals that transform everyday life, relationship with ancestors. Non-western characteristics of Christianity stand out: thinking of the Church as a family, and of faith in God through African images. Innovations in Christology are also to the fore: African communities have developed concepts of Christ the Ancestor, Christ the Healer, and other symbolic designations (just as in Asia reflection on Christ takes account of Krishna, Buddha, Muhammad, cosmic forces).

Theological output in Latin America is also many-layered and multi-faceted. Does it amount to a new paradigm, begun with the liberating option for the poor and now advancing on various fronts? There are observably several hermeneutics, as well as an overall organization. Taking the focus of this volume of *Concilium* into account – specialization in modern thought and the universal character of the Christian message – it is worth asking what the various stages of Latin American thought have contributed.

Beginning in the 1970s and maturing in the 1980s, through reading the signs of the times, the basics were reworked: salvation-liberation from sin, contextual understanding of revelation, being a community for serving humankind, and prayerful and militant rereading of the word of God. The second phase (1980s and 1990s) was more systematic. The whole situation of the poor was examined, along with the way God, Jesus Christ and mission were understood in Latin America as a whole and by specific groups. There was also a great growth in interest in and dissemination of indigenous, African-American and 'womanist' theology. These two phases might be said to have established both the basics and a holistic view. It is worth noting that there are several hermeneutics of integral liberation, the principle of which is the event of God becoming incarnate in Jesus of Nazareth, being put to death and raised to life, which transforms human beings on both the local and the universal scene.

The third phase (1990s and early 2000s) is one of a rich process open to various possibilities. Will new subjects and disciplines become increasingly specialized and move into academia, as has happened with North Atlantic theologies? Or will new structures emerge, better suited to the thought-patterns of indigenous peoples, of African-Americans, those of mixed race, women, young people, with ecological, interfaith and gender dimensions? Even among ourselves there are advances, retreats and ambivalences – hardly surprising when teaching and research institutions still treat local and Latin American concerns simply as a preliminary stage to serious reflection, or else as pastoral matters.

Despite this, there are signs of lasting and long-term progress. During the second and third phases, Christian thinking has tended to become more holistic and world-changing. Contributing to this are indigenous cosmologies, the ecological agenda, feminist and gender viewpoints, and economic and political initiatives (through various types of networks, such as those that come together in the World Social Forum). A number of individual voices stand out, though not in a self-centred way, since their epistemologies are deliberately holistic and open to one another. They do not fall into the dualism of correct/incorrect, nor do they allow themselves to be subjected to the absolutist logic of the market. Reflection in faith is rather dialogic and supportive of a full humanity, within the framework of the history of salvation.

The Latin American scene is like a concert of individual voices with universal implications. In the thriving biblical movement, communities discuss local concerns and on the basis of these fragments listen to the Word that touches every aspect of life (Carlos Mesters, Elsa Tamez, Pablo Richard). In the field of spiritual reflection on liberation, faith is authenticated through human actions (Gustavo Gutiérrez, Pedro Casaldáliga). Indigenous voices show the sacred is not opposed to the profane but rather a strength in the midst of deficiencies and always directed toward harmony (Eleazar Lopez, V. Mamani). African-American writers have emphasized the *axé* of vital energy that is at once particular and universal (A. da Silva, S. Querino). Women's voices consider daily events and relational situations as manifestations of the Spirit of God that transforms all things (Ivone Gebara, Ada-María Isasi-Diaz, Maria Clara Bingemer). The great themes of theology have been re-worked by such as José Luis Segundo, Leonardo Boff, José Comblin, Jon Sobrino and João Batista Libanio.

These hermeneutics – especially the indigenous, African, feminist and ecological ones – are forging essentially relational theological paradigms. They link the concrete and the universal and refuse to re-articulate the Enlightenment schema of the subject-object of faith. Ecological reflection joins the clamour of the earth to the clamour of the poor (Leonardo Boff). Another innovative discourse from Latin America is the meeting of religions as a basis for human and spiritual collaboration for the promotion of life (José María Vigil, EATWOT). God is not a property to be handled by churches and religions, nor is God an object of merchandise to be marketed.

Furthermore, our theological output has become more systematic since the 1990s.[9] It has been said that the Christian faith is to be understood from the essentials of the poor and their liberation (Leonardo Boff). The essentials of the poor include the mosaic of efforts to understand the Christian faith starting with excluded persons and groups seeking liberation from every form of evil. We have the challenge of reconciling fragmentation and totality. It can be said that in Latin America the ecclesial community is making efforts, from marginal fragments, to read the whole revelation of love. Our way of proceeding is not from the universality presumed a priori in North Atlantic circles but from the way the poor celebrate life. The festival of faith is like a window onto the mystery.

Particular and universal faith discourse

The theologies of the South feel themselves to be summoned by the mystery of God, and they recognize this in the signs of the times. They employ scientific studies made in each situation and at the same time take note of the wisdom of the different peoples. This implies standing back from a form of universal discourse and from North Atlantic schemas and interpretations. Such discourses are no longer normative for the South; they are by now rather ways of understanding faith that can be studied in comparison with what is done in other latitudes.

Universality is manifested in the human condition with its many faces and its common longing for happiness. In this sense, theological endeavour prefers the spiritualities and understandings proper to each human grouping, the gestation and maturation of paradigms of human interaction, and reflections that respond to the gospel of life from particular situations of our daily lives. The emphasis in our understanding of the content of faith falls on creation, the incarnation, Easter and the Church, which is missionary and the sacrament of the well-being God offers to the whole human race.

That's where we are. The theologies emerging in Asia, Africa and America look to the risen Christ, who has sent his Spirit to the whole of creation. They re-adopt the particular discourse of Jesus of Nazareth, since this is the way to universal salvation. This implies rebuilding links with a Semitic person and with an eschatological message, as well as with communities in which various cultures, social strata, personal histories and differing beliefs are present.

Christology is therefore the predominant theological output of each continent (though it is not always easy to access, given the North Atlantic bias of the publishing industry). Reflection on Jesus of Nazareth and the Christ of faith are inseparable from solidarity with the poor, with women, with all outcasts and with the cry of the earth and all its living creatures. As for meeting the Lord, his sign is our dealings with the poor and oppressed (Matt. 26.31–46). Equally specific are the community demands of those who believe in salvation without frontiers (Acts 2.42–47; 11.19–26). Stressing the details in the praxis of faith (and in the reflection that goes with it) does not imply a pragmatic approach. It is rather that we respond to the God who loves and is loved by humankind in the concrete and particular. This is the way we respond to the God who in Jesus makes himself known to every person, culture, religious body and spiritual entity. It could be said that such concrete and holistic experience is the condition that makes the theological endeavour possible.

The faith is in fact worked out in situations of suffering and injustice, from a multiplicity of forms of belief, and from a stock of hopes (thanks to the sharing of bread, to collaboration among cultures and religions, to making 'a different world possible', as the World Social Forum says). Hope springs from the groans of creation, which involves labour pains and human sighs on the part of the Spirit (Rom. 8.22, 26). In this way, concepts of an unhistorical or fundamentalist nature, which constantly assail Christian reflection, are corrected.

Another great challenge has been to dialogue with the sciences. This involves questioning them when they are co-opted by social powers, but also being challenged by them to read reality from a plurality of disciplines (without falling into fideist discourse). We also need to take on a dialogue with popular wisdoms, which are often labelled unsystematic and pre-scientific. Official sciences are particular discourses as well as popular wisdoms. The field of wisdom offers specific symbols with universal significance. The Maya civilization sees the origins of the human race being based on maize, and this enriches the Christian message on creation. In Africa, theology has for decades interacted with autochthonous spiritualities and world-views (J. Mbiti, M. Getui), while among Buddhist populations inter-religious theologians (Alonso Pieris, S. Yagi) are studying Asiatic gnosis and Christian agape, recognizing both Christ and Buddha as mediators of liberation.

Looking at theological teaching and research institutes in the developing world, we find that specialization by disciplines encourages fragmentation; this is why there are periodic demands for inter-disciplinary courses. In the past there has been most dialogue with history, economics and geo-politics; now attention is also being paid to anthropology, the arts, gender studies, sciences of religion and ecology. I see the main challenge as engaging in dialogue with the symbolic understandings of each people; for this theology needs to rediscover its mystic, wisdom and prophetic seams.

In conclusion: the ways of understanding and celebrating faith in the developing world have set out new paradigms and have rediscovered great challenges. They are taking up afresh historical responsibility (and the longing for a possible different world), the spiritual plurality with which we speak to God (instead of reifying God), and dedication to the truth that sets us free.

This is a way of thinking that conjoins the specific and the universal, the plural and the holistic. We are dealing with a theological movement progressing along two axes. On the one hand, the axis of the poor and of all who are outcast and at the same time wise; this gives priority to compassion in suffering, to action in solidarity so that there may be no more hunger or oppression. This axis is theological in its daily application. On the other hand is the difficult axis of reflecting fidelity to the Gospel of Life, incarnate transcendence, conversion from sin, the grace of salvation, collaboration among the churches for the sake of justice and peace. This second axis of the theological movement is inseparable from the first.

Forms of language, discourses, always particular and provisory, point to the universal sense of living, and they can be signs along the road toward God. Our humble discourses can be windows onto the Mystery that fills humankind and creation with joy.

Translated by Paul Burns.

Notes

1. See V. Fabella and R. S. Sugirtharajah (eds), 2000, *Dictionary of Third World Theologies*, Maryknoll, NY; L. C. Susin (ed.), 2000, *O mar se abriu: trinta anos de teologia na América Latina*, São Paulo; J. Tamayo and J. Bosch (eds), 2002, *Panorama de teología latinoamericana*, Estella; M. Amaladoss, 1998, *Vivre en liberté: les théologies de libération en Asie*, Brussels; R. S. Sugirtharajah (ed.), 1993, *Asian Faces of Jesus*, London.

2. It is clear that during the last three decades of the twentieth century new voices developed methodologies and subjects characterized by the viewpoint of the poor, to which a theological longing for a different world has been added. This involves questioning scientific, spiritual and other orthodoxies and becoming part of associations and networks with alternative world-views (the World Social Forums of Porto Alegre, Mumbai and Nairobi). Chico Whitaker has noted the emergence from the action paradigms of the twentieth century, and he regards the World Social Forums as the major political development of the start of the twenty-first century ('Les leçons d'un échec', *Foi et développement* 339:1, p. 2005). Yet academic circles in Latin America still prefer a metaphysical discourse and cite European masters; they tend to regard the new reflection as merely a pre-theology; or else they are content to admire our combination of faith, ethic and specific action.

3. E. Morin: 'The great paradigm of the West, clearly formulated by Descartes, is the disjunction between subject and object . . . a paradigm that controls completely different modes of thought . . . humanity is understood only through the exclusion of nature' (*A intelegência da complexidade*, Petrópolis, 2000, p. 67).
4. M. da Soledade da Silva, 2003, 'Sinais de Deus em nosso mejo', in Various, *A esperança dos pobres vive*, São Paulo, pp. 55–7.
5. My *La fiesta, símbolo de libertad* (Lima, 1998) is based on studies in various regions of Peru; a wider collection is M. Salinas, 2000, *Gracias a Dios que comí: el cristianismo en iberoamérica y el caribe, siglos XV–XX*, Mexico City.
6. See the final documents of the five international congresses held by EATWOT, published by DEI, San José 1982, pp. 11–26.
7. Amaladoss, *Vivre en liberté*, pp. 214, 229.
8. See E. Ikenga-Metuh, 1987, *Comparative Studies of African Traditional Religions*, Onitsha; J. Mugambi and L. Magesa (eds.), 1989, *Jesus in African Christianity*, Nairobi; J. Mbiti, 1990, *African Religions and Philosophy*, Oxford; K. Bediaco, 1995, *Christianity in Africa: The Renewal of a Non-Western Religion*, Edinburgh and Maryknoll, NY.
9. I. Ellacuría and J. Sobrino (eds), 1990, *Mysterium liberationis: conceptos fundamentals de la teología de liberación*, 2 vols, Madrid (partial ET Maryknoll, NY, and Victoria, Aus., 1993); see also the volumes of the collection *Liberación y teología*, published internationally, including twelve in English, as *Theology and Liberation*, Tunbridge Wells and Maryknoll, NY, 1990–94.

Who Framed Clodovis Boff? Revisiting the Controversy of 'Theologies of the Genitive' in the Twenty-First Century

MARCELLA ALTHAUS-REID

'The whole is always already a part.'[1]
'The question is: what should be retained and what should be rejected?'[2]

Theologies of the genitive

It was as early as 1978 when Clodovis Boff, a pioneer theologian of liberation from Latin America, considered the relation between practice and theory in liberation theology. His book from that time, *Teología e Prática: Teologia do Político e suas Mediaciones* (1978) (translated as *Theology and Praxis: Epistemological Foundations* in 1987[3]), provided an extended and informed discussion on praxis, as the epistemological base of liberation theology. One of the key elements from that discussion, which was going to influence successive generations of theologians worldwide is found in the book's introduction: 'we talk about a "theology from politics" [*teología de lo político*] and not simply a "political theology" [*teología política*]'.[4]

It is important for us to start these reflections by remembering that the context in which Boff wrote were times of political persecution and human rights violation in Latin America. The term 'political' in the context of a theological debate had then a different dimension from that found in the many North Atlantic reflections at the time. Still today, at the beginning of a new century, in some church and academic circles that dimension has been lost. And that is precisely the point. We want to start our discussion on the fragmentation of theologies in our times, not from the metaphysical perspective, structured around hegemonic interest disguised as theological crusades. The desire to preserve the so-called unity of theology against what has been called 'secular interests' only comes from those who desire power. We will ground our discussion in politics and *lo cotidiano* (everyday life) because class interests, as with racial, cultural, gender and sexual interests, are not profane interests or perspectives irrelevant to theology. At least, not for those who take seriously the incarnation of Christ in human history and are honest theologians, that is, theologians who understand that their options are informed not just by the love of God, but by less exalted interests, those formed by cultural conventions and social positions. Few distinctions have been as influential in the development of theologies of the late twentieth century as Boff's contrasting of theologies 'from' and theologies 'of'.[5]

The critique of the 'genitive theologies', as it was articulated, became the point at which the sheep were separated from the goats in political theologies, and the militant churches were separated from the churches of the status quo. First of all Boff began by defining genitive theologies as 'political theologies'. Political theologies were those concerned with particular historical practices, mainly related to the power of the state.[6] In any case, in political theologies such as the European developments from the seventies,[7] theology was always a first act. Theology never challenged its own premises and structures, and the political reality of people's lives was usually found wanting. The price of obtaining unity in Christian orthodoxy has been paid with essentialism and the universalization of historical experiences and, therefore, Christian praxis has been relegated to a minor status. Instead, Boff claimed the epistemological status of praxis.

Second, Boff along with Leonardo Boff, Gutiérrez, Altmann and others, used the term 'genitive theologies' to denounce the technique of using a mere and simplistic incorporation of new themes into current theological methods, with the resulting superficiality and inefficacy. In that sense Boff would say that a theology 'of the poor' may present 'poverty' as an added discussion, without challenging the ideological class consciousness present in Christianity, or identifying how Christian discourses may contribute or even encourage structures of poverty. Moreover, as theological fashions change (especially in these times of the market), genitive theologies tend to leave a long list of discarded themes in their wake: theologies of many themes not properly dealt with and eventually abandoned for more fashionable issues. What publishers want is novelty, and even the environment may be out of fashion now. Globalization or even new films may be considered the successful themes for today. Profit is somehow the motivation of the genitive theologies, and there are few gains (in money or respect) to be had from producing transgressive thinking. The point is that genitive theologies reflect an attitude more than a thematic, and justice and poverty usually have a relative value for these discussions.

Against that genitive model of theology, Clodovis Boff proposed then the model of 'liberation theology'. In liberation theology justice was and still is a fundamental, not a fashionable, issue from which theology arises. It is not only that the option for the poor is not an added extra to an otherwise well-developed, closed theological discourse, but the definition of politics and theology also has been challenged. In liberation theology issues of power are to be considered beyond the state, that is, on the political praxis of the *pueblo*.[8] This is a theology of the political which starts from the everyday life of Latin America, in which the actors are the destitute and marginalized. The goal of liberation theology, as with any theology of the political, is not to theologize, but to transform our societies. It is an incarnational theology and therefore a theology with agency. Latin American liberation theology, as a theology of the political, always brought the possibility of providing agency to the Christian discourse. Faith must have efficacy.

Theological fragmentations

The critics of liberation theology may consider that liberationists are responsible for the multitude of theologies which surround us, including feminist theologies, Black American, African, Asian, Aboriginal, queer, lesbian and gay: the list simply goes on and on, and even this may be incomplete. Notice that these are theologies in the plural, as each of them has variations which may exhibit agreements, differences and even contradictions. Were liberation theologies or the 'theologies of the genitive' responsible for what has been considered the fragmentation of the theological discourse of the end of the twentieth century? And where does theology of liberation stand in terms of this fragmentation, which even affects its own discourse? Let us analyse in more detail issues pertaining to the relationship of these two types of theologies.

Paradoxically, 'genitive theologies' have never been theologies of fragmentation but rather of hegemonic claims. They were exclusive theologies, each with a clear (although undisclosed) political and cultural option which sacralized, in an ideological twist, its own epistemological presuppositions. In that way, 'genitive theologies' achieved the illusion of dogmatic unity and fundamental (eternal) truth by using well-known techniques from ideological processes, such as giving divine (unquestionable) status to the origins or presuppositions of each. The single system of theological truth is preserved at the cost of theological honesty. Such critique can even be extended to European liberal theologies which may reflect on, for example, poverty, without a clear contextual engagement and a desire to produce a praxis for an alternative Kingdom in our societies.[9]

Obviously liberationists wanted more than a liberal European theology of politics. They did not want to reflect on political issues, but to change politics. A simplistic incorporation of political issues into a list of themes for reflection was seen as ineffective. It was also dangerous in so far as this approach incorporated radical calls for change into more manageable forms which could be subsumed within the structures of the status quo. Liberationists wanted a key theme such as the political to be recognized as fundamental. That is to say, poverty and economic structures of injustice needed to become the legitimate central locus for reflection, from which all other reflections would arise. In other words, while genitive theologies produced a benevolent hearing of political themes, fundamental theologies wanted structural shifts. It was not enough to 'talk about margins': what was required was a theology from the margins. Yet they did not want to fragment the theological discourse. The pioneers of liberation theology struggled for unity for a variety of reasons, including the strategic need to preserve the unity of the Church in Latin America for political reasons.[10]

That unity was not, however, a hegemonic project but rather a unity in the defence of the different cultures, economic situations, and health and welfare needs of millions of destitute Christians in the continent. Paradoxically, these Christian people were made destitute by Christianity, in the historical alliance of Church and state in Latin America since the time of the *Conquista*. However, even the theology of the political developed by the liberationists followed principles of self-limitation not so distant from those of the 'genitive theologians'. For instance Clodovis Boff warned against the 'carnival of meaning' which could arise from the reading of Scripture by the theologically untrained poor[11] if they ignored the mediating role of the Church's traditions when reading the texts. So much for Ernesto Cardenal reading the New Testament with peasants in Solentiname then![12] Even Gutiérrez's book *A Theology of Liberation* was fairly conservative by our present standards of theological enquiry. And if on issues of gender liberationists were conservative, on issues of sexuality they were still pre-modern. Liberation theology was then a theology in tension: on the one hand it was a contextual theology of rupture and engagement with critical reality, on the other a theology which could not overcome its self-limitations. Liberation theology languished in an unresolved Exodus, somewhere between the land of bondage and the promised land. Liberation theology stood somewhere between 'theologies from' and 'theologies of'.

However, as Latin American communities following the liberationist model started to raise their theological voices through a multitude of 'fragmented' theologies, certain problems occurred. There was now a feminist liberation theology, indigenous theologies (such as Andean and Maya theology) and also a new praxis, such as the crescent movement of Latin American sexual theology. In response to these developments the gap between genitive theologies and liberation theology became narrower. The liberationist orthodoxy (supported in solidarity by several North Atlantic sympathizers) has been quick to react against what it perceived as a corruption of the liberationist orthopraxis. As they saw it the fragmentation was in danger of undermining the political struggle by fragmenting the goals and objectives of those in need. If the theology from the poor is to succeed, a clear well-defined poor, as agent of change, needs to be identified in theological discourse. But if the poor happen to be women or gays, then an additional element is added to the struggle, further dividing the common front. At the very least conscientization against sexism and homophobia will have to be added to class analysis.

This issue has a history. In the early 1980s Latin American feminist liberationists were accused of two things. It was said that they sold out to the petit bourgeois claims of North Atlantic women, or that their identities were formed in the common struggles of their communities, without reference to the division of interest between male or female. Although feminist liberation theologians did not simply accept the restrictions of a so-called revolutionary theology, but developed a challenging theological praxis in their own right, it is interesting to see how (male) liberation theologians have resisted integrating into their theology contributions from other voices, such as women or Maya theologians. In a real sense the Maya, Andean or feminist theologies from Latin America became genitive theologies for liberation theologians. They dealt with them in the odd paragraph in the midst of their dense books, or referred to them in the footnotes of an occasional article. Beyond this dismissal was the fear of the fragmentation of the liberation theology project.

On hyphens and rhizomes

Several questions are posed for liberationists at the beginning of the twenty-first century. Are they surrounded by a multitude of genitive theologies which fragment the struggles of our nations, dissipating agency from their orthopraxis? Or are these theologies part of something more complex and profound? Which theology is responsible for what: is fragmentation a negative thing? Does it constitute an obstacle to the goal of social transformation? This last question is particularly difficult. In the present situation of my own country, Argentina, where the expansion of global capitalism has forced thousands of destitute families to survive by collecting refuse in the streets,[13] theology as a discourse of praxis, seeking to establish an alternative order (the Kingdom of God), cannot accept any compromise. What we pledged to defend during the 1970s as Christian theologians was that the dignity of the life of our people, the people of God, was still our priority. But that forces us to confront another type of question, that is, the possibilities of agency in theological fragmentations.

Fragmentation is a term which I have criticized elsewhere of its hidden connotations, especially the implication of a well-defined centre. Instead, let us consider a different geopolitical relationship within theology. Instead of a centre–periphery model of relations, the framework of the master and subordinate, theological thinking might benefit from making use of what Deleuze and Guattari have called 'rhizomatic' models.[14] Rhizomatic models are horizontal networks of people, institutions, thinking or theological praxis, which, as rhizomes, may network and produce connections at different levels. For instance, rhizomes could be points of connection at different sites of the struggle for integral salvation which not only produces praxis of solidarity but also an epistemological solidarity. From that perspective our liberationist praxis (our action and reflection amongst the destitute) can only grow and become more effective as new questionings and understandings come to the fore.

This is, by the way, the process by which de-ideologization occurs: the familiar and unquestioned that has been internalized needs to be identified at least to the extent of calling in question the previously taken for granted. Theologically speaking, we can only continue de-ideologizing God (or de-domesticating God, as liberationists used to call it) by exercising hermeneutical suspicion over that which precludes the possibility of revelation in the midst of our societies: the revelation of God among the scavengers of Buenos Aires, or the sufferings of the people of Colombia. The centre–periphery model, which produces the illusion of unity and dissent by presenting only two alternatives, ignores the importance of the alliances among rich nations and those excluded from our nations. The problem is that liberationists have been thinking for such a long time in terms of centre–periphery that they are unable to see that the many struggles, by gay people, women, classes and races have more than suffering in common; there is also an epistemological commonality which sustains their oppression, namely a theological one. All these theologies function with hyphens (to use a term from Lyotard[15]). These act as significant if unexpected bridges amongst each other and the project of the alternative Kingdom of justice and peace announced by Jesus. In fact, a serious reading of these theologies shows how this rhizomatic theology is developing. Feminist liberation theologians are engaging with postcolonial theologies and economic theologians are queer theologians – and vice versa. Theological identities disappear or became too complex to be easily explained. To say that a liberationist queer theologian such as myself, who works with issues primarily of class and sexuality, is 'fragmenting' liberation theology would be to accept that liberation theology is a hegemonic theology. Moreover, as new voices add new alliances of theological action and reflection, the closer we come to a model of being 'integral theologians' (paraphrasing Gramsci) instead of elite theologians.

There is no fragmentation of theologies because theology is not a unique, hegemonic project at the service of any particular interest, but an ongoing praxis of God's preferential option for the oppressed, which requires the continuous unveiling of ideological formations in Christianity and the establishment of a different model of action and reflection. In particular this means a less positivist-constructed thinking that allows different epistemological solidarities amongst the excluded, for example women, both urban and rural, heterosexuals and gay people, black, indigenous or white. Far from being genitive theologies, these rhizomatic, hyphenated theologies represent a theological project characterized by the unity and solidarity of the people of God against all kinds of injustice.

So to answer the question, 'Who framed Boff?' we need to ask who framed liberation theology, or to be more specific, which mechanisms domesticated and curtailed the subversive power of a liberating theology in Latin America. But to address that issue requires us to understand that the fear of fragments comes from the centres of power, ecclesiastical or theological, and not from the margins. Liberation theology has fulfilled its historical mission of encouraging (sometimes against its own will) this movement. It is time now that subsequent generations of liberationists realize that in the apparent weakness of different projects and theological praxis lies its strength and the possibility of continuing the preaching of the Kingdom of God with theological honesty.

In his analysis of 'the hyphen' Lyotard claimed that 'Paul's suffering, his own passion, consists in having to kill the father of his own tradition, or at least to pronounce him dead and to engender the true father revealed by

Jesus. This is the suffering of a son who needs to become the father of his father.'¹⁶ And this is also the inheritance of Latin American liberation theologians who proceed in different directions, engaging in different themes and methodologies in order to continue loving and respecting the tradition which they have proudly inherited.

Notes

1. G. Hartley, 2003, *The Abyss of Representation: Marxism and the Postmodern Sublime*, Durham and London: Duke University Press, p. 4.
2. C. Boff, 1988, *How to Work with People*, Quezón: Claretian Publications, p. 6.
3. The translation of the title of this book in English omitted the term 'Theology of Politics'.
4. C. Boff, 1980, *Teología de lo Político. Sus Mediaciones*, Salamanca: Sígueme, p. 21.
5. I am using the terms 'theologies of' and 'from' in English, where theologies of the genitive applies to a way of doing theology *for* and not *with* the people. In Spanish, and in the discourse of the pioneers such as Boff, the terms 'from' (*desde*), 'with' (*con*) and 'of' (*de*), have been used simultaneously with interchangeable meaning.
6. Boff, 1978, *Teología de lo Político*, p. 41. It is interesting to notice here the influence of Paul Ricoeur in Boff's thinking on this point. Cf. P. Ricoeur, 1953, 'Le Paradoxe Politique', *Esprit*, May, pp 729–31.
7. Boff mentions specifically the work of those who tended to use metaphysical theological subjects such as 'hope' and 'the Church' instead of real people in their discourses. Boff calls these theologies 'slogans'. Cf. Boff, 1978, *Teología de lo Político*, p. 355.
8. *Pueblo* is a concept that can be translated as people, the poor, the nation state, or even refer to ethnic groups. In Latin American theology, it is a term with strong affective connotations.
9. For this point, cf. Elaine Graham, 2002, 'Liberal Theology and Transformative Pedagogy: A Response to Peter Hodgson', in Mark Chapman (ed.), *The Future of Liberal Theology*, London: Ashgate.
10. By political reasons we mean here the need to have a church united in order to literally save the lives of the people from torture, hunger and persecution. In that sense, some Roman Catholics, Evangelicals (historical churches, including some Pentecostals and Baptists) and Jews worked in solidarity at different times. The other reasons for unity were evangelization and growth of the Church, which, for the first time in the history of Christianity in the continent, was able to gather many Christians who have been either abandoned by the established churches or too marginalized for the institution to reach them.
11. For this point, cf. C. Boff, 1987, ch. 2, 'Hermeneutical Mediations'.

12. Ernesto Cardenal wrote on his experiences of reading the New Testament to the peasants in Nicaragua, with minimum intervention, making the point that the Scriptures can not only be understood by the non-theologically trained, but moreover, their reading is illuminating. Cf. Cardenal, 1978, *Love in Practice: The Gospel in Solentiname*, 4 vols, New York: Orbis Books.
13. The *Cartoneros* (Scavengers) are a movement of dispossessed people in Argentina, who have been forced to organize themselves to survive by collecting refuse at night in the streets of Buenos Aires. For a theological reflection on the presence of God among scavengers, see M. Althaus-Reid, 2005, 'El Tocado (Le Toucher): Sexual Irregularities in the Translation of God (The Word) in Jesus', in Ivonne Sherwood and Kevin Hart (eds), *Derrida and Religion: Other Testaments*, London: Routledge.
14. G. Deleuze and F. Guattari, 1987, *A Thousand Plateaus: Capitalism and Schizophrenia*, Minnesota: University of Minnesota Press.
15. See J.-F. Lyotard, 1999, 'On a Hyphen', in Jean-Francois Lyotard and Eberhard Gruber (eds), *The Hyphen: Between Judaism and Christianity*, New York: Humanity Books.
16. Lyotard, 'On a Hyphen', p. 18.

IV. Fragmentation and Specialization: Theology and Interdisciplinarity

Theology in Relation to the Natural Sciences

PALMYRE OOMEN

In the western world the idea persists that faith (and especially the rational account of faith) is no longer possible since the emergence, and certainly not alongside the further development, of the natural sciences. Once upon a time the striking of lightning would have been seen as God's punishment: diseases, children, the harvest – everything was matter for prayers of petition, asking either to be protected from something or indeed to be blessed by it; for all of that lay in God's hand. But nowadays we put lightening conductors on the roof, we are able to understand the causes of fertility or infertility and at least up to a point to be in control of the problems related to it. We use artificial fertilizers and technologies that help us to improve the soil. We are capable of medical treatment which not only cures but also prevents diseases. The days of the God on whose will and action everything supposedly depends are well and truly over. At least that is the either/or reaction of many, and that, so they say, is also the end of theology.

But we are not finished with theology, at least not in this way. If worms – contrary to the understanding of earlier days – do not spontaneously develop out of mud, if the sun – contrary to what people used to think – does not revolve around the earth, then biology and astronomy do not cease to exist. It is the characteristic of each academic discipline that it has to come back to its original insights time and time again, and theology is no exception here. In turn, however, this also implies that theology, like all other disciplines, has to be prepared constantly to be corrected and to test previous insights critically.

In this article I first offer an analysis and an evaluation of a number of possible reactions of theology to the threat of scientific developments and influences. Following that I will speak about the sense of discomfort which efforts to bring together science and theology often generate, even for me, and I raise the question as to which are the criteria to which good theology has to do justice here. Finally I will stop and think about two connected difficulties of the enterprise 'theology and science'. I will show that these possibilities can engage with each other in a positive way thanks to the achievements of modern science and the respective philosophical reflection on them.

Theological reactions to the natural sciences

From the whole scale of theologians' reactions to the developments and influences of the natural sciences I will mention just three:[1] the reaction of conflict (which sometimes after some time may result in a limited period of harmony), the division or separation of the property, and the effort to make one's way through between Scylla and Charybdis.

Conflict

It is characteristic for this reaction that scientific knowledge and insights of faith are seen as something that is of one and the same kind, i.e. both want to describe something objectively. That is why they can end up being in conflict with each other, and that is why one must try to harmonize them. In recent centuries, theology has attempted to defend itself against scientific facts and knowledge which lead to atheism and deism by attempting to harmonize such insights with the theistic view. When this was successful, it turned out after some time that these harmonizations turned into the opposite of what they were meant to be. The English historian of science John Hedley Brooke presented this with a good sense of humour.[2] The best known embodiment of this strategy is the 'god of the gaps'. Brooke, however, presents a remarkable example of a different kind. Since the days of early Christianity the creation of the world by God has been called 'creation out of nothing'. Scientists who read this expression as a statement of information had long regarded this as nonsense: for nothing can come out of nothing. It is one of the most remarkable ideas in our time, part of the (as far as its interpretation is concerned, dark) field of quantum mechanics, that the universe could have emerged from the fluctuation of the so-called quantum vacuum (to put it simply: zero splits into minus one and plus one), so that it is said in more or less popular books with reference to science that God is not necessary for something to emerge out of nothing because the emergence of something out of nothing is simply 'natural'.[3]

In addition, Brooke shows that the arguments used by deists and secularists against the theistic perspective are equally short-lived. The French mathematician and astronomer Pierre Laplace (1749–1827), for example, showed that the solar system is able to correct itself and therefore does not require Newton's assumed divine corrections. Against this atheistic interpretation the English philosopher and historian of science William Whewell (1839) intervenes to say that if there is a mechanism for auto-correction this does not point to a lesser but rather to a greater wisdom and foresight of the creator. The Christian socialist Charles Kingsley reacted in the same way to Darwin's discovery: through the discovery of the mechanism of evolution God's wisdom comes to light in a particularly clear way. For now we can see clearly 'that he could make all things make themselves'.[4]

From this we can conclude that the arguments are less compelling than is often assumed. It is always a specific *interpretation* of scientific or theistic issues which appears to exclude the opposite view.

Division of property

Although the ideas described above still exist in many places, if not openly as conflict, still in a more subtle way as competition, they do rather have the air of goods past their sell-by date; for by now we know better: that conflicts between religion and science are frequently improper, in so far as they do not take into account the differences of genre between the two areas concerned. It has to be deemed very therapeutic to emphasize that the position of conflict is unfruitful and that religion (including theology) and science by no means have to clash. Or rather: that – with regard to their method, their interest of knowledge and their language game – they are different to the extent that in fact they cannot clash. Science aims primarily to report facts and to explain them, while the Bible does not offer factual reports and explanations, but tells stories concerning values, meaning and existence. Thus one speaks of a two-languages or two-perspectives position.

In the last century this position was strongly represented by Rudolf Bultmann (1884–1976). Bultmann argued that speaking about God's agency, just like speaking about myself as a person, implied a change of perspective. The closed chain of cause and effect is regarded as sufficient to explain fully what happens in nature and in history, so that from that perspective there is no more room for divine action or for my own personal existence. Yet I speak of myself as a person; and yet I speak of God as acting in the world. Bultmann: 'This is the paradox of faith, that faith – nevertheless – understands as God's action here and now an event which is completely intelligible in the natural or historical connection of events.'[5] This two-perspectives view is deeply rooted in the continental (and primarily in the German) philosophical tradition.

This movement in theology pays much attention to language and primarily to the different functions of language. It is stressed that alongside the informative use of speech which is characteristic for science, documentations and newspapers, there is also a performative use of speech – speech which does not primarily communicate dry information, but is able to evoke something in the hearer which appeals to feelings and a sense of value. This theological movement is less concerned with the divine origin of cosmic categories such as space and time than with a personal gracious God. It can therefore argue that one need not be schizophrenic to be at once a scientist and a believer. For those who are aware of the scientific status of the sciences understand that their subject is not 'everything'. Science and theology each have their own area of concern: science the realm of facts, the origin of the world and of reason; and theology the realm of values, the question as to how the world ought to be, and the realm of the heart. However fruitful it may be for the awareness that many conflicts need not exist, this distinction between the 'truth of faith' and the 'truth of reason' has a number of inherent difficulties. In locating the relationship between God and the world exclusively in humanity, theology has to a large extent encouraged a godless understanding of the physical world. Wolfhart Pannenberg rightly argues that theology has not turned away unpunished from the task to think through modern scientific thought and to deal with it; for as a consequence of this turning away a chasm has developed between the thinking about the physical world and the Christian faith. The result is that an atmosphere has developed which regards it as one of the imperatives of intellectual integrity not to take into account Christian ideas in this area.[6] Thus the world becomes God-less and God world-less (Moltmann).[7]

Searching for commonalities while respecting genre differences

Is it really the case that God has something to do with the areas studied by the sciences? Yes, for theology is concerned with 'everything' *sub ratione Dei*, according to the classical understanding of theology with which I concur here.[8] This means that basically all finding of truth, whether in the area of psychology or cosmology, of history or mathematics, of physics or in the social sciences, in biology or ethics, is of interest to theology. Essentially this means that theology will not do justice to its obligation to offer a multi-faceted and all-encompassing view of humanity and the world in relation to

God if it completely ignores the relationship between God and the material world.

In addition to those who stress the difference and therefore agree to a 'division of property', there are thus also those who stress that such a division is not really possible in hard and fast terms. No matter how different facts/being/existence/reason on the one hand and values/meaning/faith on the other may be, there have to be, so they argue, points of contact between them.

The point of view of this third position can be described in the following way: in order to be good theology, theology is required to include in its thinking about the physical world those things which we hold as true about God and the world. In doing so it must not relapse into the naive one-dimensionality of the position of conflict. In other words: the difference between the genres (which are strongly emphasized by the 'division of property' model) ought surely to be honoured, but not (as is done by those who argue for 'division of property') in order to use this genre difference as an argument for no longer relating both areas to each other.

Characteristic of this third position is the view that theology cannot without negative consequences ignore one of the two sources: 'Scripture (and Tradition)' and 'Nature'. If we look only at Nature God is only discussed as an impersonal principle on the meta-level of law (or not even there). If on the other hand we look only at Scripture, what is left is only the God of sense and meaning, separated from the hard physical facts with which we are faced day by day. In this way God becomes world-less and thus irrelevant.

Thus both sources must be taken seriously. This, however, does not prevent our recognizing that both sources are not easily harmonized. We may not be naive, for there is an awareness of brokenness on both sides. Scripture is God's self-revelation through human understanding and shaping and error. Likewise nature is not the immediate product of God's creation, for nature is God's creation through natural processes and influences. If we say that theology has to engage with science in one way or another, we are by no means finished. On the contrary, this is where the problems begin!

A sense of embarrassment and the question of theological standards

Where theology and science are in conflict with each other we regard this as out-dated. Where they ignore each other, this is unsatisfactory, at least for theology. But – where they enter into a new relationship and produce books with titles such as *God and Quantum Theory*, *Did Jesus Also Die for Extra-*

terrestrials? and *Can Computers Sin?*, this generates a sense of embarrassment. How are we to assess this sense?

The embarrassment can simply arise from the fact that what is offered here is a new language and a new context. However, 'new' or even 'strange' need not be interpreted as 'wrong'. This is even less true since the sense of embarrassment is at least in part no more than the expression of that which we had always known, that the two areas of theology and science had grown apart.

Furthermore it is characteristic of interdisciplinary studies that they touch on more than one area of knowledge (e.g. physics and theology, frequently supplemented with the required mathematics and philosophy, which is or is not part of it). Faced with so many areas of knowledge one is not easily able to become an expert in all of them. The sense of embarrassment can in any case also be a useful warning signal, that one could be led up the garden path, or without knowing could be making a category mistake.

The sense of embarrassment could also be of a more theological nature. With regard to a number of the problems and solutions described above we have the strong sense: this is no good, this is speaking about 'God' but not theology, or this is not the way in which theology should formulate the question, let along solve it (just look at the word 'solve'). This raises the urgent question whether there are standards, and what they are, which our efforts to engage theology and science with each other must live up to.

It should be self-evident that interdisciplinary studies would only make sense if the different disciplines concerned can be involved each on their own level, i.e., on the level of our knowledge in the respective area as it is today. With regard to interdisciplinary studies in the borderlands between science and theology this would mean that the science as well as the theology and philosophy would need to be 'up to date'. There must not be a connection between very advanced contemporary scientific insights with theological-philosophical thinking which has not gone through the 'turn to the subject', the 'linguistic turn', the criticism of metaphysics and modernity (and the criticism of those criticisms). Likewise we must not relate contemporary theological awareness with now outdated scientific and philosophical insights with regard to causality, determinism, time, space and so on.

This formal criterion enables us to have immediate insight into some of the fundamental difficulties of a relationship between theology and science. I name only two of them: first of all, the effort to relate theology and science easily creates a theory where God is introduced as a producer of explication (e.g. for the fact that there are laws of nature and laws of nature of this or that particular kind at that). The question thereby raised is whether the fact that we mention God within the sphere of 'explanation' does not mean a relapse and whether it does not imply that we are not doing justice to the criterion formulated above.

Second, theology of the twentieth century is profoundly marked by secularization. Is speaking of God (not just in relation to humanity but also) in relation to nature not a rejection of the secularized cultural climate and thus a way of speaking that falls short of the achievements of contemporary theology?

Exploration of these difficulties and emerging possibilities

I want to go into some more detail with regard to these interconnected objections, as they are the reason for much discomfort and much disapproval with regard to 'science and theology' literature. But I also want to do so to show that, if looked at more closely, it is precisely these points which offer possibilities for fruitful reflection about the relationship between theology and science.

God and causality

Even if we don't want a 'division of property' between science and theology, with the former aimed at explaining and the latter at understanding, there remains one particular difficulty with regard to the relationship between theology and scientific explanatory thinking. For explaining means to search for causal connections, and the relationship between 'God and causality' is a massive problem.

From a schematic point of view there are two possibilities for combining God and causality. The first is that God functions as an explanatory factor in order to fill the gap which would otherwise remain in the chain of explanation. For example, we do not know how in the process of evolution the 'spirit' came into play, and then we say: 'This is a particular divine intervention.' As we have already seen, this need for God in order to be able to close the chain of causality rapidly turns into rendering God superfluous. Thus theologians are very hesitant about seeing God as the one who is needed as a factor inserted to provide an explanation. Furthermore, and more principally, one is reluctant to have God, if regarded as such a 'factor between the factors', demoted to the level of finite things, this being inadequate in the light of God's transcendence. It is for these strategic and principal reasons that theology rejects such a 'God of the gaps'.

The second possibility is connected with the fact that causes do not always have to be on the same level. For example, the answer to the question 'Why does the apple fall from the tree?' could be 'Through gravity.' The potential following question, 'Why does gravity exist?', is of a higher order. It is generally the case that scientific explanations involve the ordering of particular cases under general laws, and the finding of such laws. The questions 'Why is this law as it is?' and 'Why do laws exist in the first place?' are not part of science. It is to this second category of questions, the so-called meta-questions, that scientists who are believers, or theologians who engage with science, easily answer with 'God'. Theology, however, is reluctant to move God exclusively to the meta-level as this means that God's existential concern with the here and now disappears entirely.

The question is whether if we speak about God in the context of our reflections on causality, these are the only alternatives: either 'here and there in between' or 'everywhere on a meta-level'? I don't think so. For these alternatives are based on a mechanistic understanding of causality which among other things means an understanding of causality in which causes form a closed chain (or net) and of necessity have an effect as a result. This mechanistic concept of causality was already sharply criticized in the philosophical reflection on the natural sciences during the early twentieth century (e.g. by Charles S. Peirce or Alfred N. Whitehead); *inter alia* because it was not longer able to take sufficient account of new scientific discoveries (from electromagnetism, field theory or evolutionary biology). Furthermore the findings of quantum mechanics have triggered a broad discussion about causality, which *inter alia* has led to ideas of ontological indetermination, i.e., the idea that causal switches might not be closed. Yet a further impulse comes from the reflection on information whereby the possibility of an influence of information comes to the fore. All of this suggests that there may be many more concepts besides the two we have mentioned, to use in relation to the influence of God – also concepts in which openness, value orientation and indeterminist ontology are possible.

Thus the mathematician, scientist and philosopher Alfred Whitehead developed as a reaction to the deficiencies of mechanicism an indeterminist ontology. In it he describes 'what really is' as an event. It is an event which syntheticizes itself out of its causal influences. Here it is essential that the causal influences together in their entirety are not entirely determining. In this ontology we not only hear of physical causes, but also of a criterion which renders one possible development more desirable than the others. Under the influence of this difference with regard to attraction, an event can orient itself and really happen.

The vision of the quantum physicist and theologian John Polkinghorne shows (at least in this point) much similarity and is likewise founded on an ontological openness of all events. Polkinghorne develops this in the sense that processes are not entirely determined by their physical causes but that alongside these physical causes there is also the influence of a 'pattern-forming active information'.

In still another way the biochemist and theologian Arthur Peacocke founds his thinking about God and causality, on the 'top-down causality' by which a whole influences its parts. We may also mention the model of the theoretical physicist David Bohm who speaks of a non-local connectivity related to what he describes as 'implicate order'.[9] Here I am merely concerned with showing that the mechanistic thinking in terms of causality in science is so thoroughly debated, that perhaps the time is ripe to revise the theological received truth, that we ought not to think about God in terms of a 'cause'. Thus, speaking about standards and rules of the game, the game has already started . . .

Secularization

In speaking about God in the context of physical reality we seem to lapse very rapidly into massive, realistic and materialistic speech about God. However, in our secularized culture we can no longer speak about God in this way. Is the 'Theology and Science' enterprise then not a neglect of cultural sensitivity, a cultural sensitivity that has found its precipitation in present-day philosophy and theology. This question is relevant in the light of the criterion we have already claimed, that the intended integrative studies on the part of science as well as on that of theology or philosophy must be up to the present level of knowledge.

One problem is that the hard, substantivist understanding of being ('things that objectively exist', 'real things that exist independently of others' etc.) are placed within science, while we regard existential being, ways of being which imply being a subject, being which is constituted by meaning, as the domain of the humanities and within them as the domain of theology. However, such an attribution of roles is largely outdated. If the naive understanding of reality is being tested anywhere it is particularly in the physics of the late nineteenth and twentieth century. We only need to mention here the 'field theory' according to which 'mass' and 'bodies' are secondary phenomena, that is, concentrations of energy in restricted locations and points within a field. We can also mention matter, which together with 'anti matter' is generated out of 'nothing', which of course is not a real 'nothing' but a 'quantum vacuum' 'structured by the laws of quantum mechanics and the equations of the quantum fields involved';[10] particles which have the characteristics of waves; particles which can go through two slits at once, or rather 'entities' which do that and only take on the characteristics of particles when they are observed. It is precisely modern science that shows that 'reality' is not the same as 'naive objectivity' (Polkinghorne). Modern science in particular shows that, for theology, conversations with science can be particularly fruitful if together with secularized culture it wants to get away from a massive, objective speaking about God!

In conclusion

Having arrived at this point we can say that the formal criterion – that the science concerned as well as the theology concerned have to be brought up to today's level – has been elaborated here with regard to some of its material concretizations for theology. The conclusion which can be drawn with regard to these points, issues of 'causality' and 'secularization', is that theology which seeks to deal with some of the results of modern science will not inevitably fall back behind its own achievements and that – to put it in positive terms – it will in some points find affirmation for precisely these achievements.

Thus surprisingly it also becomes obvious that the norms which theology has to apply for itself are not fixed a priori, but also depend on the philosophical interpretation and elaboration of developments in the sciences. As a result this leads to the idea that not everything can be ensured a priori and from the sideline. The finding of the way is partly due to being on the way.

Translated by Natalie K. Watson based on the German translation by Ansgar Ahlbrecht.

Notes

1. Here I rely indirectly on Ian Barbour's four types, i.e. conflict, independence, dialogue and integration. See Ian G. Barbour, 1997, *Religion and Science: Historical and Contemporary Issues*, San Francisco.

2. John H. Brooke, 1989, 'Science and the Fortunes of Natural Theology: Some Historical Perspectives', *Zygon* 24:1, pp. 3–22.
3. Polkinghorne rightly remarks, having mentioned the fact that physicists from time to time refer to the effects of this quantum fluctuation as '*creatio ex nihilo*': 'There is no area in which the interaction of science and theology is more bedevilled by theological ignorance on the part of the scientists than on the discussion of the doctrine of creation.' John Polkinghorne, 1998, *Science and Theology: An Introduction*, Minneapolis, p. 80.
4. Brooke, 'Science and the Fortunes of Natural Theology', p. 18.
5. Rudolf Bultmann, 1983, 'The Meaning of God as Acting', in O. C. Thomas (ed.), 1983 [1958], *God's Activity in the World: The Contemporary Problem*, Chico, California. (The author's original text is in English.)
6. Wolfhart Pannenberg, 1970, 'Kontingenz und Naturgesetz', in A. M. K. Müller and W. Pannenberg (eds), *Erwägungen zu einer Theologie der Natur*, Gütersloh, pp. 33–80, here 36f.
7. Jürgen Moltmann, 1985, *Gott in der Schöpfung: Ökologische Schöpfungslehre*, Munich, p. 28.
8. Cf. Thomas Aquinas, *Summa Theologiae* I, q. 1, a. 7.
9. See M. Hulswit, 2002, *From Cause to Causation: A Peircean Perspective*, Dordrecht e.a.: Kluwer; A. N.Whitehead, 1978, *Process and Reality: An Essay in Cosmology* [1929], New York: Free Press; Polkinghorne, *Science and Theology*, esp. p. 89; A. Peacocke, 1993, *Theology for a Scientific Age*, enlarged edn, London: SCM Press, esp. pp. 53–5, 373–4; D. Bohm, 1985, 'Hidden Variables and the Implicate Order' and 'Response to Conference Papers', *Zygon* 20:2, pp. 111–24, and pp. 219–20.
10. Polkinghorne, *Science and Theology*, p. 80.

Theology and the Social Sciences

RICHARD H. ROBERTS

Dramatic and ongoing changes in the world configuration of economic and political power since the collapse of the former Soviet bloc have been accompanied by a significant and differentiated increase in the socio-cultural significance of the religious factor at both a global and local level. Correspondingly, as intimated by the editors of this issue of *Concilium*, Christian theologies have undergone a process of differentiation. In this contribution I do not intend to rehearse the history of that diversification but to adopt a strategic response informed by tenure of professorial chairs at the opposite extremes of British reflection, in a highly traditional theological faculty and in the first department of religious studies in the United Kingdom, respectively. In short, I am seeking to interpret a complex shared context of interpretation, not to emphasize arbitrary polarities.

The extreme managerialization and commodification of all British higher education and its reconfiguration into a system of mass human production, a veritable cloning of predetermined 'quality' identities, has had profound, but little understood, consequences for the living, researching and teaching of Christian theology and the training and control of ministers and priests, as well as for the academic study of religion. In this context all forms of employment that involve a sense of vocation are in potential or actual crisis in the face of the untrammelled power of managers to redefine the identities of employees. We live, as the American sociologist Willard F. Entemann has argued, in the era of 'managerialism' that succeeds the economic historian Joseph Schumpeter's triad of 'capitalism, socialism and democracy'. This extreme, indeed quasi-sovietic centralization in Britain has led some to conclude that new spiritual and theological life will have to grow on the margins and in the interstices of the societal monolith that is 'managerial modernity'.[1]

This latter is a highly explicit form of social construction, in the face of which social scientists, scholars in the humanities and theologians have found refuge in theory and in displaced shared discourses of survival.

Theology and the Social Sciences

Indeed any significant deviation from the enforced protocols of 'quality' in teaching and learning may well abort a potential career.

Historical context: from secularization paradigm to the resurgence of religion

Given this context, what follows is an attempt briefly to map out some of the conditions of a creative encounter between theology and the social sciences. This is on the assumption that 'theology' as the relatively autonomous and critically reflexive discourse of any given tradition must relocate its activity in the matrices of the social and human sciences (*les sciences humaines, die Geisteswissenschaften*) if it is to meet the challenges with which it is confronted. In general terms, and for the most part, the post-Enlightenment history of the relationship between theology and the social sciences has been that of separate development, a situation institutionalized by the separation of theology from humanities faculties in those modern universities that followed the example of the founding of the University of Berlin in the early nineteenth century.

After the Second World War, French Catholic '*sociologie religieuse*' pioneered the quantitative empirical study of religion and changes in religiousness, and this provided the international bedrock for the emergence of European and then North American sociology of religion in the post-war period. There was thus a major flowering of this sociological subdiscipline from the late 1960s through to the mid-1990s led by (for example) such figures as David Martin, Bryan Wilson, Roland Robertson, Barbara Hargrove, Michael Hill, Milton Yinger, Charles Glock, Ronald Stark, Peter Berger, Steve Bruce, Karel Dobbelaere, Roland Campiche, and so on. Central to the work of this generation and of their pupils has been the progressive refinement of theories of secularization, based on the assumption that religion was in terminal retreat in the face of modernization, and that, in the final analysis, this process was final and irreversible. It is now apparent that this consensus has proved less than a satisfactory interpretative response to the increasing and often problematic salience of the religious factor in the world system.

The global 'resurgence' or 'return' of religion as seen in, for example, radical conservativisms and fundamentalisms, religiously inspired terrorism, the syncretic religiosities of 'New Age' and the therapy culture, the revival of ethnic and religious nationalisms in the aftermath of the collapse of Marxist socialism, has challenged the adequacy of the traditional sociology of religion as grounded in secularization theory. Moreover, there have been important theoretical developments in mainline social theory, such as the emergence of the modern/postmodern problematic, extensive reflection on the reality and significance of globalization, debates on the adequacy of social constructionist theory, the central role of the 'risk society', and the fuller emergence of environmental and ecological perspectives. Taken together, these all amount to a new context that has yet fully to be absorbed into the social-scientific study of religion, never mind theology.

Retrenchment in theology and reductionism in religious studies

Meanwhile, a dominant trend in formal Christian theology has been retrenchment into post-liberal postures advocated by such figures as the French Catholic theologian Jean-Luc Marion and the lay Anglo-American Anglican John Milbank.[2] The present Archbishop of Canterbury, Dr Rowan Williams, has trodden a careful path in which adherence to what Marion conceives as the central theological role of the bishop has been allied to a careful refusal (as opposed to Milbank) to dispense with the theological *ancillae* of the social and human sciences. These strategies allow Christian theology to persist as a self-authenticating cultural-linguistic practice free from the contamination of what Milbank has depicted as the 'heretical' discourses of the social and human sciences. They do not, however, allow theology to address the real question of holism in a differentiated world. Beyond mere theory this requires an approach in terms of the evolution of a 'human ecological' understanding of societal as well as environmental sustainability. The adoption of such a perspective implies re-engagement with repressed, displaced and marginalized transformatory processes now rampant in the psychotherapy/spirituality interface.

Confronted by these apparent polarities the field of study represented in Anglo-America by 'religious studies' might at first sight afford grounds for a resolution of the distancing of theology and social science, but closer examination yields a situation parallel to that of the sub-discipline of the sociology of religion. The latter tends to reduce the object of inquiry to the effects of social construction, through, for example, the application of rational choice and marketing theory to religious and spiritual commitments. Within the multidisciplinary field of religious studies the phenomenological method pioneered by such figures as Ninian Smart has been attacked as culture-specific and has given way to debates about the viability of the category 'religion' itself on both philosophical and postcolonial grounds. Central to some of the more strident sectors of religious studies is the quest for the unholy grail of the final reductive scientific explanation of residual religiousness. A concomitant rejection of human universals of the kind upon which the unitive vision of Mircea Eliade in large measure depended has tended to paralyse any ability on the part of religious studies practitioners to address the political, ethical and environmental implications of their field of study. This situation has consequences similar to what happened to analytical philosophy once it deconstructed its substantive remit and became merely the critic of the injudicious linguistic ploys of other disciplines, the discourses of which logical analysts presumed to clarify. In such an unpromising environment it is not surprising that the subtle public intimations of religion, religiousness and a/theology associated with the discernment of the 'shadow of spirit' and the 'after-life of religion' apparent in post-structuralism and the 'condition of postmodernity' became attractive to elite intellectuals in the humanities, while the academic religious professionals have often become trapped in self-stultifying and sterile debates.

The study of religion and main-line social science

The history of the socio-scientific study of religion is of course intimately connected with the Enlightenment project, the onset of industrialization, the fate of 'lost defeated tradition' (Alasdair MacIntyre) and the growth of the disciplines of the human and social sciences in the nineteenth century. Both early anthropology and sociology of religion have to be understood against the background of a growing legitimation crisis which was itself (in contrasting ways) a central concern of the 'founding fathers' (Marx, Weber and Durkheim). The subsequent isolation of the religious dimension (and not least theology) from central issues in social science is one consequence of the role that the analysis of religion played in the development of the thought of these key figures. The relative isolation of the empirical study of religion (later formalized in the 'history of religions' and the 'phenomenology of religion', and the disjunction between anthropological and sociological approaches (concerned with 'culture' and 'society', respectively)) were rationalized in a variety of ways. Now, however, societal transformations and their theorization (including those aspects of both that may be construed as 'religious') demand a new construal of the religious field. In the remainder of this paper we outline core elements of such a strategic response.[3]

As noted above, secularization theory has been the central issue in the sub-discipline of sociology of religion throughout the post-Second World

War period in Europe and North America. It is apparent that secularization as theoretical construct has had implications which pass way beyond those of the sociology of religion understood as a sub-discipline of sociology. Thus Marx, Weber, Durkheim and Simmel, and in recent decades, Foucault and Blumenberg opened up perspectives that extended the frontiers of secularization theory on to the broader plane of the interpretation of both high and popular culture. Within the sub-discipline itself, adherence to the secularization paradigm nonetheless became something close to a test of disciplinary orthodoxy.

A further central issue in the traditional sociology of religion has been the continuing analysis of the Weberian 'Protestant ethic' thesis. This extended discussion has not only been enlarged in the direction of 'economic cultures' (as by Berger, Martin, Roberts and others) but also been opened up so as to include the discourse of religion, that is, to draw into consideration the 'theologies' which specifically seek to endorse, or to undermine, such cultures (as by Michael Novak and the American neo-Conservatives, as opposed to Clodovis and Leonardo Boff and others). These factors may then be understood in the context of main-line discussions of the nature of 'capitalism' and economic systems which have been thought to require a cultural and ethical base for their effective working.[4] Here, however, any arbitrary dichotomy between sociological and anthropological research methodologies is increasingly problematic. At the core of managerial society 'spirituality' is increasingly exploited as a means of securing changes in core human identities and the securing of reality acceptance. The suffusion of both religious and quasi-religious phenomena by commodification and marketization can, under certain conditions, reduce 'spirituality' to a new and instrumental 'spirit of capitalism'. Here it is important to discern and map distinctions between 'resource' and 'capital', between the use, exchange and intrinsic 'values' of 'religion', 'the sacred' and their cognates.

Once having undercut the hegemonic and interest-driven theory of secularization, renewal of method in the socio-scientific study of religion demands a re-examination of the relation of religion to the diverse construals of 'modernity' to be found in main-line sociological and cultural theory. Traditional sociology of religion has largely subsisted on the basis of repeated recyclings of its relationship with the 'founding fathers' (i.e., Marx, Weber and Durkheim) and largely outdated conceptions of 'modernity'. By contrast, contemporary main-line sociology, anthropology and cultural studies have broadened their foundations. Thus a typology of the 'modernities' now in current discussion (e.g. by Anthony Giddens, Ulrich Beck,

James Beckford, Scott Lash, Brian Turner, John Coleman, Alain Touraine, Pierre Bourdieu and so on) may serve as the basis of an initial reconfiguration of the religious field. It is apparent, however, that such reconstruals are both strongly affected by the socio-cultural impact of modernity and post-industrial or advanced capitalism, and provisional in the light of interpretations of the postmodern problematic itself. Central, however, to contemporary modernity are the managerialism, risk calculation, predominance of 'expert systems' and surveillance in which new cultural contradictions emerge, and in the context of which religious and spiritual factors undergo multiple transmutations. Most theology is ill-equipped to respond to such a complex matrix of social construction.

Mainline theoretical responses to the social construction of religion

Basic questions concerning the nature and meaning of 'religion' are not, however, confined to debates within religious studies. The progressive marginalization of religion associated with the phenomena of de-traditionalization, the differentiation of spheres, pluralism, and so on, identified with the secularization and 'Protestant ethic' paradigms, have induced what was in effect a 'colour-blind' approach to a range of factors that now emerge, even within the confines of the paradigms themselves. By deriving theoretical input from outside the inverted and ghettoized settings of both theology and the sociology of religion, it is possible to re-conceive the religio-spiritual impulse. So, for example, the late Pierre Bourdieu's integrated theory of culture as 'capital' on the basis of a combination of both sociological and anthropological insights helps us move from the consideration of marginal religion in the shadow of 'modernity' to its interpretation as a live and active factor in the context of the 'condition of postmodernity'. Religion and religiousness are one element, albeit distinctive and highly differentiated, within the global and local system of the use and exchange of culture. These realities are contested, paradoxical and ambiguous, both indispensable and risk-fraught. The religio-spiritual principle is intrinsic to the ancestral, even primordial tasks of deep socialization – and manifest in surrogate forms as it migrates and transmutes under modern and postmodern conditions.

One example of this transmutation can be observed in the career of the church/sect typology inherited from the classic works of Weber and Troeltsch and strongly developed in the post-war period (by Bryan Wilson and others) that first required modification in order to account for the continuing existence of sectarian groups and 'cults'. The dominant outlook assumed the marginality of such phenomena, religion was usually regarded as peripheral, a declining force in a fully secularized world. Social movement theory, which had gained momentum from studies of the origins of National Socialism and the Third Reich, and then later Communism and McCarthyism, had largely independent origins. Later, however, the emergence during and after the 1960s on a more societally significant scale of a wide range of new religious movements (NRMs) precipitated extensive research (e.g. by Eileen Barker, James Beckford, David Bromley and Meredith McGuire). A partial convergence between the sociology of religion and the study of social movements took place, initially through the mutual application of resource mobilization theory. Later a more specific convergence of theoretical perspectives is apparent (in, for example, the work of Beckford and Touraine). Yet more recently, organization theory (as, for example, in the work of Stewart Clegg and a range of management theorists) provides key points of entry into the analysis of contemporary religious change.

Furthermore, the widespread tendency to regard religion as a substitute for political action and/or deviance born from dispossession (a reflection, not least, of pervasive Marxist influence) has been challenged by the growth of (for example) activist Pentecostalism, liberation theology (both in the late 1970s and 1980s) and Islamic fundamentalism in Iran and elsewhere in the late 1980s and 1990s. Religious fundamentalism is of course a global phenomenon apparent in Christian, Jewish, Muslim and Hindu forms. The construction of a typology of the interpretations of global fundamentalism (by, for example, Gilles Kepel, Martin Riesebrodt, and the Harvard project) is again best undertaken in relation to theories of modernity rather than to the secularization paradigm. The global and cross-cultural character of fundamentalism requires consideration in terms of globalization theory.

Globalization theory (as traced from Sergei Eisenstadt, through Immanuel Wallerstein to Roland Robertson, Manuel Castells and others) has important relevance to the task of interpreting the global and local relationships between religious belief systems and ethical values on the one hand, and the global economy and trans-national business (and thus business ethics) on the other. Roland Robertson's post-Marxist globalization theory proposes a far more substantial role for beliefs, values and practices in the world system than that allowed for by the secularization paradigm. In reaction to the economic determinism of recent thinkers (and also as reflected in much popular thought), globalization theory can controversially attribute substantive importance to religious and ethical values in the world system, although, for some, of a reactive character. Such values may, however, be seen to have a more than merely epiphenomenal role and status: the renewal of interest in religion as a substantive factor capable of social agency, as a force for potential good in a globalized world as proposed by Robertson, or as a more reactive response according to Peter Beyer. Under globalized and virtualized conditions, it is paradoxically the case that a quasi-theological vocabulary of practical omniscience and instantaneity becomes the sole discourse capable of representing the magnitude of societal transformation. Social theory and theology are thus (despite the cordon sanitaire of the theological 'Radical Orthodoxy') inextricably and perhaps unwillingly connected in a struggle for representation. Sociologically speaking, globalization provides the setting for the discussion of interlinked aspects of identity crisis, those of the nation and nationalism, and of individual and of group or community identity, respectively.

In the complex setting sketched out above, 'culture' has become an essentially contested concept. 'Cultural studies' problematizes and thematizes the life-worlds of late modernity and thus functions as an inexpensive surrogate for a reflexive anthropology. The decline and reconstrual of 'class' analysis in terms of relative cultural deprivation and the emergent importance of 'identity theory' once more relates the interpretation of religion to current developments in social and cultural thought, drawing, in particular, upon social psychology. The crisis of identity is, however, informed by two further factors. These are the postmodernization of social and cultural conditions and the emergence of feminist and gender theory, both of which now exert constitutive influences upon the contemporary religious field as much as they have influenced theology.

Conclusion: religion and theology in the modern/postmodern matrix

Adequate social-scientific study of religion in the modern/postmodern matrix will (at the very least) demand consideration of five interlinked key headings that amount to socio-cultural transcendental categories of contemporary social reality. First, the emergence of the postmodern problematic implies the transformation of space and time. Second, given the feminist critique of patriarchy, gender theory has precipitated a reconfiguration of concepts of the deity. Third, the flight into virtuality and cyborg enhancement becomes a dangerous and illusory response to the 'end of the human' and imminent environmental catastrophe. Fourth, the foregrounding of self, body and radical immanence is evident in contemporary spiritualities. Fifth, the contested genealogy of 'charisma' and the juxtaposition of ancestral and postmodernizing cultural factors in the debate on 'primal religion', global shamanism and techniques/technologies of ecstasy confront both the theologian and the social scientist with the transformatory power of the religio-spiritual impulse.[5] A renewed Christian theology will have to engage in dialogue with, rather than evade, this complex recomposition of the religio-spiritual field.

Notes

1. See R. H. Roberts, 2002, *Religion, Theology and the Human Sciences*, Cambridge: Cambridge University Press. This book contains an exhaustive bibliography.
2. See John Milbank, 1989, *Theology and Social Theory*, Oxford: Blackwell.
3. What follows is based upon my research and teaching on religion and social theory in the Department of Religious Studies at Lancaster University since 1995.
4. Here the British example is interesting: in a multicultural society lacking any moral consensus, surveillance and managerial control demanding total transparency under the unquestionable hegemony of the 'Performative Absolute' are regarded as more desirable than residual reliance upon reflexive trust or the acquisition of values.
5. See R. H. Roberts, forthcoming, *Critique of the Social-Scientific Study of Religion*.

Saving Doctrine: Towards a Theology of Health and Medicine

STEPHAN VAN ERP

Theology and medical science share an interest in human well-being. Both academic disciplines deal with matters of life and death, and of responsibility and communication at times when people's existence, their trust and their vulnerabilities are at stake. Yet, theology's dealings with medicine are generally restricted to medical ethics and to pastoral theologies of care in nursing homes and hospitals. Thus, theologians have missed the opportunity to reflect systematically upon situations that everyone will have to deal with at some point: becoming ill, caring for others, and being dependent on the care of others. In these circumstances, people's lives become intertwined with narratives of sin, suffering and salvation. Why do we get ill? How do we view illness and health? What are the politics, the aims and limits of care? Doctrinal theology should be concerned with these questions to be of service to practical and moral theologies, but also to medical practice. Moreover, it is a worrying fact that systematic theologians have been ignoring matters of health and medicine. By means of analogy, it makes one wonder about the function of a chapel or meditation room in a hospital: a place to get away from all the misery, to find comfort in isolation and silence. Theology should articulate that silence, surely, but in the face of pain and sickbeds, and not away from it all.

In this article I would like to argue that medicine is not only a matter for moral and practical theologies, but also a source and workplace for systematic theology. Confronted with illness and disease, medical doctors, nurses, patients, pastoral carers and family members all apply their views – explicitly or implicitly – to their work and care. To understand the task of doctrinal theology to articulate, compare and contrast these views, I will first clarify the connection between religion and medicine. I will then describe the modern split between religion and medicine and the current failing attempts to restore the connection. Finally, I will sketch a theological agenda for future research on medicine and health.

The ancient covenant between religion and medicine

Religion and medicine have been closely connected throughout most of human history. From the Mesopotamian blend of supernaturalistic (rituals) and naturalistic (herbs) medical treatments, and the ongoing tradition of North-Asian shamanism to the modern Christian pilgrimages to Lourdes, there has always been a close relation between them.[1] It would however be misleading to put it that way, since it suggests the connection consists of two distinctive realms or cultural forms that overlap in certain situations. In fact, very often this has not been the case, and religion and medicine have been inextricably intertwined. Artefacts from the pre-dynastic period in Egypt indicate that mental illness and physical illness were both understood as caused by evil spirits and demons. The writer of Psalm 38 laments that 'there is no soundness in my flesh because of your indignation; there is no health in my bones because of my sin'. Until this very day, some still regard epidemics as the act of divine retribution, and many more think illness and disease result from the disfavour of God. I would even dare to suggest that the question 'Why me?' when someone has become critically ill, even when posed by a non-religious person, manifests at least anticipated traces of a transcendent plan or decision.[2] This in turn has led Susan Sontag to attempt freeing contemporary culture from the combination of illness and punishment – its religious origins and its fatalistic character – in her famous essay 'Illness as metaphor'.[3]

Will modern medicine and its biomedical approach eventually cure us from these last traces of religion, which seem to run through our veins like an intractable infection? Or does it confront us, despite – or should I say thanks to – its impressive and astonishing successes, with human longings for health, the meaning of suffering and sickness in society, and the limits of curing and caring for others? If the latter is the case, and I would like to suggest that it is, then medicine could be a source for rethinking religion and for rediscovering doctrinal views on sin and suffering, and on healing, wholeness and salvation, in other words, medical practice could be a source for rediscovering religious doctrines, that is, theology. To understand how medicine could be considered a theological source, the 'and' between religion *and* medicine first needs clarification.

The key text of western medical practice, the oath of Hippocrates (460–377 BC), comes across as surprisingly secular in its description of medical actions and responsibilities, although the oath used to be addressed to 'Apollo the physician, and Aesculapius, and Hygieia (Health), and Panaceia

(All-heal), and all the gods and goddesses'. Its pragmatic tenor made sure this oath survived as a founding text for medical doctors throughout modernity, unlike for example the oath and prayer of Maimonides (1135–1204), the medieval Jewish philosopher and rabbi, whose text is imbued with explicit religious language. The oath genre of both texts signifies at least the public nature of medical practice. Its continuing performance until today stresses the safeguarding of that practice as a communal responsibility through the individual response to the call to enjoy the art of medicine. But does it still manifest the religious character of that call or of the profession? By removing the addresses of the original version of the Hippocrates' oath and not replacing them by an alternative, modern medical doctors who take the oath not only want to make clear that they do not live in the same culture as the Greek polytheists, but also that their work is accountable to secular authorities alone rather than deities. Does that signify the end of the long-lasting relation between religion and medicine? And should it be considered as the victory of modern medical science over religious interference in medical practice?

It is undoubtedly true that the rise of modern medicine is the product of scientific results and not of religion. Especially when medicine is concerned, I would say that science justifiably has put religion in its right place. But the history of Christian theology itself has always shown a very ambiguous relationship with medicine, putting it at the forefront of the life of faith, but also questioning or at least nuancing it from the very beginning.

The early Christians regarded their responsibility to care for the sick and the poor – be they Christian or non-Christian – as ultimately religious. According to some, this has led to one of the profoundest contributions of early Christianity to western culture, which has lasted until the present day and hopefully will last much longer: organized medicine for all.[4] Medical care was taken to be one of the main religious tasks, a case of worship and prayer. This view was inspired by texts such as James 5.14–16:

> Are any among you sick? They should call for the elders of the church and have them pray over them, anointing them with oil in the name of the Lord. The prayer of faith will save the sick, and the Lord will raise them up; and anyone who has committed sins will be forgiven. Therefore confess your sins to one another, and pray for one another, so that you may be healed. The prayer of the righteous is powerful and effective. (NRSV)

From a Christian perspective illness and disease were initially related to sin, and healing to the effects of confession and prayer. From the fourth century onwards Christian-inspired medical practice became connected with physical healing as well. From then on both caring and curing were seen as core religious acts, expressing and performing the life of faith through the confession of sins, prayer and eventually also through what we now call 'biomedical practice'.[5]

This close relation between medical and religious practice of the early Christian Church – and there are similar connections in non-Christian religious traditions – could easily lead to misunderstandings, such as that the sick are sinners by definition or that prayer will heal us from our illnesses. Both misunderstandings are based on an all too neat identification of religion and medicine, and on the idea that religion could be applied to manipulate our health. This idea has become very popular again and despite it being supported by sound and scientific qualitative research, there are good theological reasons to deny it, and both Scripture and the history of Christian theology provide enough arguments to do so.

Basil the Great (329–379), for example, warned against the disproportionate valuation of health and healing in view of faith:

> When we were commended to return to the earth whence we had been taken and were united with the pain-ridden flesh doomed to destruction because of sin and, for the same reason, also subject to disease, the medical art was given to us to relieve the sick, in some degree at least.

And he continues:

> Whatever requires an undue amount of thought or trouble or involves a large expenditure of effort and causes our whole life to revolve, as it were, around solicitude for the flesh must be avoided by Christians.[6]

Basil's remarks show that however central the acts of caring and curing may have been to the life of faith, they have also always been understood as the modest and humble participation in the ever-greater scope of God's salvific and redemptive work.

Already in Romans 8.18–23, we find the idea of healing set in a more eschatological tone:

> I consider that the sufferings of this present time are not worth comparing with the glory about to be revealed to us. For the creation waits with eager longing for the revealing of the children of God; for the creation was subjected to futility, not of its own will but by the will of the one who

subjected it, in hope that the creation itself will be set free from the bondage to decay and will obtain the freedom of the glory of the children of God. We know that the whole creation has been groaning in labour pains until now; and not only the creation, but we ourselves, who have the first fruits of the Spirit, groan inwardly while we wait for adoption, the redemption of our bodies. (NRSV)

From science to instrumentalism: the rise and fall of modern medicine

Despite biblical and theological arguments against a direct causal relationship between faith and healing, the history of Christianity has accommodated much medical quackery that suggested that the individual victory over sickness would be the effect of the 'true' life of faith. Contrary to current proofs that individual spirituality cures, medieval and early modern 'proofs' were less convincing if not harmful, and modern science provided medicine, especially in the nineteenth and twentieth centuries, with major achievements and progress. In view of their failing predecessors and supported by their own successes, the practitioners of modern medicine have warned against a disproportionate valuation of religion in health and healing.[7]

Besides becoming a culturally honoured practice founded on modern scientific results rather than on insights derived from faith, the rise of modern medicine has had two other consequences in relation to religion. First, medicine and health seem to have become fetishized as Feuerbachian deities, in so far as we project most of our hopes and desires concerning life and death on them. As such, the practice of medicine has become a cultural and political force of high significance, and apart from the abuse that that usually attracts, it has increased the devastating impact of medical failures and mistakes.[8] Second, medical science seduced religious scholars into submitting their ideas of religion and spirituality to the same type of instrumental reasoning and ideals of achievement.

The emergence of fetishizing medicine and health as the replacement – or should I say prosthesis of the covenant – between religion and medicine, could be described as a culturally constructive and religious act in itself, instead of as merely the result of modern medicine. Stephen Toulmin has argued that medicine has challenged radical individualism, because of its focus on the human condition that we all share.[9] Furthermore, he has described medical actions as the result of relationships between individuals and between individuals and society, rather than as the alleviation of individual pain alone. Max Weber interpreted this communal dealing with suffering in view of religion when he investigated the idea of theodicy in his *The Sociology of Religion*:

> the more the development tends towards the conception of a transcendental unitary god who is universal, the more there arises the problem of how the extraordinary power of such a god may be reconciled with the imperfection of the world that he has created and rules over.[10]

And he continues, following the results of a questionnaire submitted to German labourers, that it 'disclosed the fact that their rejection of the god-idea was motivated, not by scientific arguments, but by their difficulty in reconciling the idea of providence with the injustice and imperfection of the social order'.[11]

So, according to Weber, religion functions in society as the either failing or convincing explanation of suffering on the one hand, while on the other it shows that different belief systems create different societies through their explanation of suffering. Subsequently, he states that suffering as a social experience is the foundation and function of religion in society. Understanding the 'and' in religion *and* medicine is primarily an exercise in hermeneutics.[12] It asks for the ongoing clarification of the presuppositions and constructive meaning of ideas on sickness, suffering and health, and of the practices of caring and curing.

Current research on religion and medicine, however, seems to have fully and uncritically adapted to the pragmatic idea that religion and spirituality have an important functional influence on medical practice. This is shown by the number of academic publications on the theme, which has grown exponentially in recent years. A selection of searches in the medical science database Pubmed/Medline on query combinations like 'spirituality and health' or 'religion and health', returns thousands of publications, mainly from the last decade.[13] The scholars performing these research projects are mainly medical anthropologists and psychologists, who in general do not work in a faculty of theology or religious studies.[14] It is also important to note that most publications deal with spirituality rather than religion, and that most articles on spirituality deal with either non-western religious traditions or the topic of coping, and then again, most of the articles on coping are on prayer. So, current (Anglo-American) research in religion and medicine shows a tendency towards ethnography, individualism and instrumental rationality.[15]

Theologian and medical ethicist Stanley Hauerwas has argued strongly against an instrumental approach to the study of religion and medicine and the cultural idol of the therapeutic. In an article on suffering, he fights the assumption that the task of medicine is to relieve suffering. According to him the danger lies in the idea that medicine will eventually be used as a tool to alleviate every form of suffering, while only pain can be alleviated and suffering is something to endure rather than to eliminate.[16] Furthermore, there is the danger of the idea of an instrumentalized deity. Apart from the fact that Hauerwas could be criticized for making an all too clear distinction between bodily pain and mental suffering, or for making ethics the religious guardian at the limits of medical practice, he puts his finger on the sore spot by showing the lack of theological reflection in the case of instrumental reasoning.[17]

Towards a theology of health and medicine

Should a theology of health cure the new field of research of religion and medicine from its instrumental rationality, by offering what Giambattista Vico (1668–1744) in his *Scienza Nuova* paradoxically called a 'medicine for science': revealing and practising a new poetic way of seeing, thinking and writing, as an alternative version of modernity? Or, to put it in Milbankian terms, could a theology of medicine provide a counter-discourse to what could be seen as the impoverished, narcissistic and self-deluding scientific-technological rationalism of the modern age, violating the bodies of individuals and society? I would suggest, instead of a counter-discourse to sidetrack modernity, there is need of a systematic theology conversing with the current practice of medicine and the medical sciences. Such a conversation would be searching for answers to the problems of modernity instead of establishing an academic competition in search of human well-being.

To start such a conversation between theology and the medical sciences, a phenomenological description of experiences of and views on illness and disease is needed, so that these can be analytically compared and contrasted. In doing so, it will become clear that beyond phenomenology, theology provides for a tradition of reflection on the hermeneutics of experience, which relates experience to culture, tradition and interpretation. Especially when addressing the idea of suffering, which concerns the whole person and not just the body, it will become manifest that neither a neutral description of suffering, nor a resignation to individual experience or mere opinion will suffice to understand suffering, let alone to confidently support certain medical decisions.[18] The combination of the phenomenological description and the hermeneutics of experience will show that health and medicine, besides dealing with curing, caring and alleviating pain, are also concerned with ideas, views and theories – in other words, with doctrines.

Furthermore, a hermeneutical approach will relate individual experiences and opinions to the social and the political. In the case of health and medicine, the articulation of the communality of experiences of suffering is an urgent task. This is not only the case because dealing with illness and disease requires transparent communication between doctor, nurses and patients, or because health and medicine have a cultural impact. The influence of politics and policies of hospitals and nursing homes on medical caring and curing and their responses to medical consumerism is also important for furthering cultural and communal awareness in the medical sciences. Much work on this level has been done already.[19] Nowadays, an increasing number of medical faculties appoint professors of public health. Medical anthropologists have recently been developing an ethnography of experience, articulating that suffering is a shared, interpersonal experience.[20] But theologians and other scholars in the field of religion are well equipped to take part in this debate, being able to offer their expertise on the historical and socio-cultural meaning and meaninglessness of pain and suffering, and of sickness and health.

Entering the debate on the meaning of pain and suffering, and of health and medical care, is perhaps the most important contribution of theology to an interdisciplinary conversation about medicine. Apart from sharing concerns about individualism, therapeuticism, instrumentalism and consumerism, theology and religious studies have their specific tasks in this conversation. The Christian doctrines of creation, incarnation and salvation, when carefully and enthusiastically explained to medical scientists, undoubtedly have something to contribute to the ideas of health and care, if only to articulate the givenness of life and the politics of belonging to the people of God. Moreover, as I have shown before, an oversimplified connection between sin and suffering could be refined with arguments from Scripture and the history of theology.

But the specificity of the theological conversation with medicine does not have to limit itself to the Christian narrative, if 'narrative' is defined as the history and identity of Scripture and tradition.[21] It could also add to the conversation a certain sensibility for that which Rowan Williams, referring to Michel de Certeau, has described as 'what brings to speech that absence which makes possible the shifting space of prayer and witness that is Christian life'.[22]

Responding to that sensibility and confronted with the instrumentalism of medical reasoning and research into the effects of spirituality, theology could kenotically utter the sound and be the voice of the sick and the sufferers. Not through the resignation to either the positivism of science by following the same patterns of approach and achievement, or the fatalism of a misunderstood concept of spirituality without resistance, but through the search for an understanding of suffering as a shared – that is, historical, social and cultural – experience and through compassionate presence. Thus, theology has the opportunity to rediscover and enter the tradition of care and healing through the conversing confrontation with contemporary medical practice. That way, medicine could be viewed and experienced as the space in which traces of the divine can be encountered.

Notes

1. 'A History of Religion, Science and Medicine. Historical Timeline', in H. G. Koenig, M. E. McCullough, D. B. Larson (eds), 2001, *Handbook of Religion and Health*, Oxford, pp. 24–49; cf. P. Rioresci, 1995, *A History of Medicine*, Omaha.
2. Cf. W. H. R. Rivers, 1924, *Medicine, Magic and Religion*, new edn, 2001, London, esp. pp. 1–26.
3. S. Sontag, 2001, *Illness as Metaphor and Aids and its Metaphors*, New York.
4. G. B. Ferngren, 1995, 'Early Christianity as a Religion of Healing', *Bulletin of the History of Medicine* 66, pp. 1–15.
5. Cf. H. G. Koenig, D. M. Lawson, 2004, 'Religion and the Long Tradition of Caring for the Sick', in H.G. Koenig and D. M. Lawson (eds), *Faith in the Future. Healthcare, Aging, and the Role of Religion*, Radnor, pp. 98–110.
6. Basil the Great, 'The Long Rules', in *Saint Basil: Ascetical Works*, trans. M. Wagner, 1962, Washington, p. 331.
7. Cf. R. Porter, 2005, *Flesh in the Age of Reason*, Basingstoke.
8. Cf. J. W. Bowker, 1997, 'Religions, Society, and Suffering', in A. Kleinman, V. Das, M. Lock (eds), *Social Suffering*, Berkeley, pp. 359–81.
9. S. Toulmin, 1982, 'How Medicine Saved the Life of Ethics', *Perspectives in Biology and Medicine* 25, pp. 736–50.
10. M. Weber, 1971, *The Sociology of Religion*, trans. E. Fischoff, London, p. 138.
11. Weber, *The Sociology of Religion*, p. 139.
12. A similar case has been made by Bowker, 'Religions, Society, and Suffering', p. 363.
13. http://www.pubmed.gov
14. For similar query experiments, see Koenig et al. (eds), *Handbook of Religion and Health*, 6, pp. 513–90.
15. For an example of instrumentalism, see J. Levin, 2001, *God, Faith, and Health:*

Exploring the Spirituality–Healing Connection, New York. For a criticism of instrumentalism, see E. Biser, 'Kann Glaube heilen? Zur Frage nach Sinn und Wesen einer therapeutischen Theologie', in B. Fuchs and N. Kobler (eds), 2002, *Hilft der Glaube? Heilung auf dem Schnittpunkt zwischen Theologie und Medizin*, Münster.

16. S. Hauerwas, 1986, 'Reflections on Suffering, Death and Medicine', in *Suffering Presence: Theological Reflections on Medicine, the Mentally Handicapped and the Church*, Notre Dame, pp. 23–38.
17. Cf. Jürgen Habermas's criticism of instrumental rationality in J. Habermas, 2002, *Religion and Rationality: Essays on Reason, God and Modernity*, Cambridge.
18. Cf. E. J. Cassell, 2004, *The Nature of Suffering and the Goals of Medicine*, 2nd edn, Oxford.
19. For example, M. Little, 1995, *Humane Medicine*, Cambridge.
20. A case that has recently been made by medical anthropologists: A. Kleinman, J. Kleinman, 1991, 'Suffering and its Professional Transformation: Toward an Ethnography of Experience', *Culture, Medicine and Psychiatry* 15, pp. 275–302.
21. Cf. J. J. Shuman, K. G. Meador, 2003, *Heal Thyself: Spirituality, Medicine, and the Distortion of Christianity*, Oxford.
22. R. Williams, 2005, 'God', in D. Ford, B. Quash, J. M. Soskice (eds), *Fields of Faith: Theology and Religious Studies in the Twenty-First Century*, Cambridge, pp. 75–89, 81.

Theology: Discipline at the Limits

ERIK BORGMAN

Everyone working in a university is aware that he or she is involved in an institution which is increasingly fragmented. Compared to the traditional idea of a university as an organization mirroring the organic unity of all fields of knowledge and learning, it makes sense to speak of a 'university in ruins': what we have are the fragmented remnants of an organic whole that have become autonomous.[1] Academics are caught, as W. David Shaw, emeritus professor of English from Victory College, University of Toronto expresses it, between 'Babel and the Ivory Tower'.[2] Babel of course stands for the cacophony of paradigms, approaches, points of view and styles of thinking and reasoning in today's academia, and the ivory tower stands for the specialized, idiosyncratic research of the individual scholar in his or her brilliance. But, as in the biblical story, the Babylonian confusion of tongues is closely related to the building of a 'tower with its top in the heavens' in order to make a name for ourselves 'lest we be scattered abroad upon the face of the whole earth' (Gen. 11.4). According to the story in Genesis, God's response to this longing to stay united by conquering the power of heaven results in the human race scattered upon the earth and fragmented into a myriad of languages and points of view.[3] The Christian story of the coming of the Holy Spirit at Pentecost suggests that the reconciliation of the tensions and conflicts that come with plurality does not necessarily lie in returning to the lost unity. We should speak in such a way that everyone hears the truth in their own language (cf. Acts 2.8).

In this article I will defend the thesis that in a pluralist culture, theology is not the restoration of the unity of the world our culture – academic and otherwise – has supposedly lost, using the word of the God who in essence – 'Hear, O Israel' – is One. Theology is a discipline at the limits of academic disciplines and other organized and established systems of reasoning and knowing. It is theology's task to deal with these limits and to deal with the fact that they are experienced as limits that have, in a sense, already been exceeded. Ultimately, it is theology's mission to discover ratio and order beyond all disciplinary limits, a ratio and order on which the disciplinary forms of rational thought and research ultimately live. This implies that, counter to common belief in academia in the western world, theology is not losing its ground and relevance because of the advancement of other disciplines and sciences. The growth of knowledge does not make theological questions obsolete, but confronts us with new theological questions. One of the most important of these new questions is how the plurality of insights, explanations and understandings that are undeniably enriching our knowledge but also enlarging the field of our uncertainty and lack of knowledge, are related to the truth as the object of human longing which the Christian tradition ultimately identifies with God.

Incomprehensible reality

In an important essay for *Concilium* with the intriguing title 'On Naming the Present', David Tracy in 1990 showed not so much how the plurality of attempts to understand the present are potentially complementary in aiding a proper and unambiguous understanding of the 'signs of the times', but how in their irreducible plurality they show the impossibility of unambiguously naming the present.[4] 'We live in an age that cannot name itself', is Tracy's very first sentence. Tracy does not see this as a flaw in our capacity to comprehend, but as a characteristic of the present that refers to itself as postmodern. Thus it shows that one is only capable of saying what it is not, and not what it is – a phrase that in itself already suggests that there is a relationship between the incomprehensibility of the present and the incomprehensibility of God as expressed in classical negative theology: we can only say what God is not, not what God is. During the last decade or so David Tracy has been involved in what he himself called (1999) 'recovering the hidden and incomprehensible God' as especially significant for a time – but also, it seems to me, especially accessible in a time – which discovers its own essence as hidden and incomprehensible'.[5]

With all its stress on hiddenness and incomprehensibility, this thesis implies a certain view on religion and the religious traditions, which is linked to the analogical view on the contemporary situation. For religion this view implies that its function is not to solve the ambiguities of the present, our lives, life and history in general. Religion is a way of dealing with this ambiguity, a way of understanding the significance of these ambiguities. For contemporary culture it means that it is seen as religiously and theologically significant not where it presents questions that the religious traditions in general and the Christian traditions in particular can answer, but where it opens itself up as signifying and expressing a mystery. Where culture shows that it is a way of partially grasping what in the end escapes every grasp, it presents itself as a revelation of – the title of David Tracy's 1999/2000 Gifford Lectures and reportedly also of his forthcoming book – *This Side of God*. Thus, the object of theology is not simply the Christian tradition or people's religious practices, but all traditions and practices and the world that they speak and act in, together making for the contemporary situation. This is particularly important to stress where theology tends to be seen either as a rival to other disciplines, losing battle after battle whenever others succeed in understanding, explaining and comprehending the reality we inhabit and are ourselves, or as a discipline studying religion and its traditions. In the view I here relate to David Tracy – which I earlier also related to other Catholic theologians in the *Concilium* tradition such as Marie-Dominique Chenu, Yves Congar and Edward Schillebeeckx, and with the Second Vatican Council's Pastoral Constitution *Gaudium et Spes*[6] – the situation itself has theological characteristics, pointing to the hidden and incomprehensible God.

Here it is particularly important to realize that this means that the plurality of disciplines and the way of dealing with them can in itself be regarded as a theological issue. Roughly two-and-a-half millennia after 'the discovery of knowing',[7] we seem to be in a situation in which we do not know what we know of our world. We cannot name its truth. Instead, we are confronted with a wide variety of approaches, intellectual traditions and research strategies, and what they produce as insights. This forces us as theologians to acknowledge that our own tradition is but one among many, also implying that theology as a discipline is not one, but multiple. David Tracy has always put pluralism at the very centre of his theological projects.[8] In the 1980s he concentrated on the question of how the pluralism of contemporary culture affects theology that is traditionally so strongly focused on unity and order as an image of the Divine. In his more recent work, however, he seems to discover pluralism as not just a problem for theology, but as having theological significance in itself. As early as 1987 with his *Plurality and Ambiguity* Tracy's pluralism points to difference, to the necessity of conversation and discussion, to the need for interpretation and the uncertainty that comes with it. The more we know, the more what we know is part of a larger whole of unknowing. This witnesses to the fact that reality always remains a mystery, related to God who is, in the phrase of the German theologian Eberhard Jüngel, 'Geheimnis der Welt', mystery of the world.[9] David

Tracy never related this in a systematic way to the plurality of academic disciplines and its theological significance, nor did anyone else. At the interdisciplinary Heyendaal Institute for theology, sciences and culture at the Radboud University in Nijmegen, the Netherlands, we are in the process of starting a project to analyse and evaluate interdisciplinary practices and understanding them theologically. In my reflections here on Tracy I am developing a starting point for this project.

As noted before, dealing theologically with the vast plurality of different academic disciplines does not mean trying to restore the supposed unity of a past Catholic or Christian world-view. It means first of all accepting the plurality of academic disciplines, sub-disciplines, methodologies and approaches as the contemporary way of organizing our knowledge of reality. As in many confrontations with contemporary culture, 'kenosis' is a key concept for theology here. In the spirit that was in Christ Jesus (cf. Phil. 2.5), theology has to empty itself of everything that puts it above the other disciplines, for instance because it claims to deal with God and therefore to speak in the name of *id quo maius cogitari nequit*. According to the Christian tradition God's highness is hidden in what is low and seemingly without prestige and glory.[10] But in the very fact that the fragmented production of knowledge is seen as the *kenotic* presence of the human longing to know the truth and live in its space, the limits of the scientific and academic disciplines are also revealed. Not in order to come to an easy, but therefore ultimately empty, criticism of their forgetfulness of the fundamental source or ultimate goal of reality, but in view of a constructive critique that rescues that which tends to be forgotten, but always remains present. It can never be the mission of theology to introduce God into reality, not even the reality of academic research. Theology's mission is always to find God's hidden presence and, in the case of the current 'university in ruins', to show that in this presence the unity of reality we long for is already given, be it in a hidden way.

Therefore, especially interesting from a theological point of view are the instances where disciplines in their isolation are confronted with their limits. Important are the moments and places where it becomes clear too that in order to find their way forward and increase our knowledge further, they have to get into contact with other disciplines, to experiment with new methodologies, to look at what they do with different eyes. That makes interdisciplinary research a possible *locus theologicus*. Not because where other disciplines are confronted with their limits, theology can supply answers beyond these limits, but because in interdisciplinary research the ultimate impossibility to comprehend and master reality from one point of view comes to light. Theological traditions do not tell us what we should think about reality, but challenge us to focus on where reality shows its mystery and to explore what happens there. The logic within each academic discipline or sub-discipline is to stay away from its limits, and to focus on what can be researched within these limits. In its traditions, theology treasures ways of dealing with the incomprehensible, with the truth that is always withdrawing and never simply present. It suggests that it can be extremely worthwhile to reflect on and to come to know about what is principally hidden and beyond our comprehension.

Rationalization versus rationality

We seem to be living in the world Max Weber predicted early last century.[11] On the one hand, our culture is thoroughly rationalized, just as every part of our reality is scientifically explored and there is no separate field of knowledge that can integrate and connect the fragmented and fragmenting knowledge produced by the academic disciplines. Just as in our theoretical reflections an all-compassing world-view has disappeared, in practical life our orientation does not come from any grand narrative any more. We pragmatically reflect on the situation as it is and project the situation we wish for ourselves and those we feel connected to. From there we scan reality as it is for available means and realistic, reachable ends. This rationalization of our lives in terms of means and ends has brought us a historically unique level of prosperity, gives us a life expectancy previously unknown and brings cultural goods formerly reserved to the elite within the reach of many – although we also tend to be too forgetful of those from whom they are still withheld, in the Third World but also within the societies of the western world. But just as the rationalities of the academic disciplines and sub-disciplines are confronted with their limits, the rationality of means and ends shows its limits too. Modern societies in the West are characterized by a high level of dissatisfaction and frustration. People are experiencing a fundamental lack and long for a truly good life. What this good life is, is hardly articulated, and one could argue that a major crisis of the western world is that it is increasingly unable to discuss the question of what a good life might entail, and this limits public discussions to technical questions on how to reach most efficiently certain set goals. In Max Weber's analyses, modern society becomes an 'iron cage' that calls forth the will to escape. But the mainstream political expressions of this will paradoxically lead to the further enhancement of the bureaucratic rationality that led to the experience in the first place.

Max Weber predicted that as an effect, people would try to escape from rationalized societies by cultivating all kinds of forms of irrationality. What we see today could to a large degree be interpreted as cultivating irrationality: excessive expectations and dreams for one's life, lacking any relationship with what can be realized; violence and alcohol and drug abuse, attempts to forget temporarily the responsibility to lead a rationally ordered life in excessive behaviour among peers during rock concerts or sports matches. And maybe the most problematic form of irrationality, because it is so hard to notice: the broadly shared conviction that long-time and difficult problems should not be part of our lives and our societies. Rational thinking and responsible behaviour should no longer be necessary, according to many people. The ideal is to live in a situation in which whatever is done spontaneously, is good. In Max Weber's sociological framework this kind of behaviour is understandable but totally irrelevant to the course of history. It is useful for people's psychological well-being and helps them to cope with the social situation of ongoing rationalization that unavoidably is and stays ours. With rationalization we continue to build an iron cage, in Weber's view: without rationalization civilization will end and we will fall back into the absolute chaos of irrationality.

Theology suggests that there is a third possibility here. The Christian tradition teaches us to focus exactly on what escapes the rationality of means and ends, to try to hear the message present in the longing that has no place in the dominant rationalizations. Liberation theology in its different and multiple forms has done and does exactly that. It tries to follow the God who in the words of the apostle Paul chose what is foolish in the world to shame the wise, chose what is weak in the world to shame the strong, chose what is low and despised in the world, even things that are not, to bring to nothing things that are (1 Cor. 1.27–28). While doing this, liberation theology never stops arguing rationally. It tries to understand what the longing to escape the current rationality of means and ends has to say to us in rational terms. Liberation theology attempts to break away intellectually from the thinking that excludes what cannot be thought about in terms of available means and reachable ends. It focuses on the longing that cannot be rationalized and therefore marks the limits of the current rationality, and – to use the enlightening distinction Stephen Toulmin has made between rationalism and reason – tried to show what is reasonable in this longing and in its light.[12]

In our modern societies, rationalized in Weber's sense, the view on science has become extremely constructivist. Rationality is seen as coming from the disciplined ordering of things, not from a hidden or even repressed order in reality itself. In the current epistemologies and philosophies of science, science is not understood as investigating the order of things, but as ordering things in such a manner that they can be investigated. Theologians should challenge this view on reality, not by criticizing scientific research practices in an abstract way, but by concentrating on the limits of the academic disciplines and sub-disciplines. These are also the limits of scientific construction. Liberation theology concentrates on the limits of the current social logic, convinced that wherever this logic is challenged, a vision of a new, liberating logic could be dawning: the logic of what Jesus according to the synoptic Gospels called the 'Kingdom of God'. In an analogical manner theology should in the midst of other disciplines concentrate on the limits of the current scientific and academic logic. This implies on the one hand a clear awareness that any order of thinking excludes a great deal in order to suggest its all-compassing character, an awareness that is convincingly articulated in postmodern theories. On the other hand, concentrating on the limits of the current academic disciplines only makes sense if on these limits new ways of being reasonable present themselves and new forms of rationality are in the process of revealing themselves. This means breaking away from the typical postmodern concentration on the antinomies of modern rationalization and actively hoping for and exploring the possibilities of a rationality-beyond-rationalization.

Because Jesus suffered outside the gate of the current society, those who follow him must also 'go forth to him outside the camp', as the author of the New Testament letter to the Hebrews writes, 'bearing abuse for him'. For instance, they had to bear the mocking of the pagan philosopher Celsus, who in the third century AD ridiculed the Christians for leaving behind 'the teachers of civilization, the sensible and the Father himself', to find the true life lessons in 'the women's quarters, the leather shop and the weaving mill'. The theological tradition tells us that God as the ultimate Truth is also the creator of heaven and earth who left traces in his creation. Making an effort to suppress temporarily my inclination towards modesty, I would suggest that theology should remind the academic disciplines that their ultimate responsibility is not to their methodology or their rationalizing approaches, but to what traditionally is called 'the Truth'. That Truth is present in our day and age as the kenotic awareness that however much we know, reveal and comprehend of reality, its hiddenness and incomprehensibility are always bigger. And what we know, reveal and comprehend takes its value and meaning from the fact that there is a part that remains hidden and incomprehensible. In other words: all our knowledge can best be understood as the – necessarily partial and limited – knowledge of reality as an encompassing mystery.

A theological project

Theology has always had to deal with the fact that its object – for classical theology that is God – is beyond comprehension in our limited attempts to rationalize reality. Theology could help the academic community to reflect on what it means not to be in charge of the object of one's discipline and to be led by it to new situations fundamentally beyond our imagination as long as they have not occurred. Re-styling theology as a reflection on the mystery of the Hidden, the Incomprehensible and the Impossible – again using David Tracy's words – in the situation we are part of and live in, means opening new possibilities for theology. I even dare to say that understanding theology as reflecting on the necessity of developing multidisciplinary and interdisciplinary research beyond the limits of the given and developing disciplines and sub-disciplines, means also rediscovering theology as theology.

Breaking away from the classical tradition, Friedrich Schleiermacher in his *Der christliche Glaube* (1821–22) redefined theology. For Schleiermacher the subject matter of theology was no longer God, but the beliefs of the Church. From knowledge of and reflection on a hidden and incomprehensible reality classically called God, theology became thinking about and discussing the beliefs and convictions people had and have about God. The concentration on the human faith in God has been growing ever since in theology. As a consequence, if it is at all considered an academic discipline, theology is currently seen as one of the ways to study religion. Theology does not study religion in a neutral, existentially detached way as phenomenology of religion and religious studies are supposed to do, but is engaged in an attempt to contribute to the future of religion and a particular religious tradition. Whatever may be the reasons to restyle theology thus, it should be clear that it puts us in danger of losing an important feature of classic theology. Classically, theology considers religion not simply as one aspect of human life – although it is of course also that, and did increasingly become that during the development of modernity and its functional differentiation of the different spheres of life: a form of behaviour different from for instance economic or political behaviour – but as an revelation of what is fundamental to human existence, even to existence in itself. When religion is studied as a phenomenon distinct from other cultural and anthropological phenomena, it is easy to lose sight of the claim of at least the Christian religion that the God it worships is the creator of heaven and earth and the end of history. Therefore, this God is relevant to everything human beings say, do, feel and think inside or outside the religious sphere, regardless of their being believers or not.

According to the classical definition of Thomas Aquinas, theology is speaking about everything. It is not just speaking about religion, and neither is it speaking about God as if God was an object distinct from but comparable to other possible objects of human knowledge. According to Aquinas, theology speaks about everything *sub ratione Dei*, under the aspect of God. Concentrating on where the academic disciplines become aware of their own limits in grasping reality, revealing how the ongoing growth of knowledge notwithstanding, reality remains a hidden and incomprehensible mystery and in a sense becomes ever more hidden and incomprehensible because of our growing knowledge, can be understood as a translation of the classical *sub ratione Dei*. Theologically speaking, these limits reveal what David Tracy calls 'this side of God' as – in the classical definition of the relation between God and the analogical way we know God – in every likeness with the knowledge we have of it through the academic disciplines always being more unlike this knowledge.[13] One could make substantially the same point by saying that the religious character of scientific knowledge is rediscovered that way.[14] The academic disciplines may have thought for a while – and often still tend to think – that they are based on and produce certainty. However, they discover over and over again that they are ultimately based on uncertainty, that their knowledge comes into existence in dealing with the hidden and the incomprehensible and as part of the hidden and incomprehensible. And dealing with what is hidden and incomprehensible, but at the same time fascinating and demanding our dedication to reveal its mystery, is a major characteristic of the religious.

That this can lead to exciting new multidisciplinary and interdisciplinary research will hopefully become clear in the near future. I am convinced that it will also become clear that this can lead to a new understanding of God: a God who is hidden and incomprehensible, but who is revealed in the dilemmas, the uncertainties, the limits we experience and want to overcome but have to live with. God is known in not just the longing for, but also the practising of the impossible and unexpected that constitutes our lives.

Notes

1. Cf. Bill Readings, 1996, *The University in Ruins*, Cambridge MA and London: Harvard University Press.
2. Cf. W. David Shaw, 2005, *Babel and the Ivory Tower: The Scholar in the Age of Science*, Toronto, Buffelo and London: University of Toronto Press.
3. Ellen van Wolde, 1994, *Words Become Worlds: Semantic Studies of Genesis 1—11*, Leiden: Brill.
4. David Tracy, 1990, 'On Naming the Present', *Concilium* 26:1, pp. 66–85; reprinted in David Tracy, 1994, *On Naming the Present: God, Hermeneutics and Church*, Maryknoll: Orbis Books, pp. 3–24.
5. D. Tracy, 1999, 'Form and Fragment: The Recovery of the Hidden and Incomprehensible God', Palmer Lecture – see <http://www.ctinquiry.org/publications/reflections_volume_3/tracy.htm>
6. See my '*Gaudium et spes*: The Forgotten Future of a Revolutionary Document', *Concilium* 41:4 (2005), pp. 48–56, and 'Truth as a Religious Concept', *Concilium* 42:2 (2006).
7. For the expression 'the discovery of knowing', cf. the title of the history of sciences by Chunglin Kwa, 2005, *De ontdekking van het weten: Een andere geschiedenis van de wetenschap*, Amsterdam: Boom (The Discovery of Knowing: A Different History of Science).
8. Three of Tracy's major books have the word 'pluralism' or 'plurality' in their title or subtitle: cf. his, 1975, *Blessed Rage for Order: The New Pluralism in Theology*, New York: Seabury Press; 1981, *The Analogical Imagination: Christian Theology and the Culture of Pluralism*, New York: Crossroads; 1988, *Plurality and Ambiguity: Hermeneutics, Religion, Hope*, London: SCM Press, 1988.
9. Cf. Eberhard Jüngel, 1977, *Gott als Geheimnis der Welt: Zur Begründung der Theologie des Gekreuzigten im Streit zwischen Theismus und Atheismus*, Tübingen: Mohr.
10. For the importance of *kenosis* in the confrontation of theology and other disciplines, see the brochure Philip Clayton wrote, invited by the Radboud University in Nijmegen at the occasion of the retirement as a member of this board of Jan Peters, also president of the *Concilium* foundation: Philip Clayton, 2005, *Critical Faith: Theology in the Midst of Sciences*, Nijmegen: Radboud University.
11. Cf. M. Weber, 1904–05, 'Die protestantische Ethik und der Geist des Kapitalismus', in Max Weber, 1988, *Gesammelte Aufsätze zur Religionssoziologie* I, 9th edn, Tübingen: Mohr, pp. 17–206, here pp. 203–6.
12. Stephen Toulmin, 1990, *Cosmopolis: The Hidden Agenda of Modernity*, New York: The Free Press; 2001, *Return to Reason*, Cambridge MA and London: Harvard University Press.
13. '. . . inter creatorem et creaturam non potest tanta similitudo notari, quin inter

eos maior sit dissimilitudo notanda': H. Denzinger, 2001, *Encheridion symbolorum, definitionum et declarationum de rebus fidei et morum*, 39th edn, no. 806.

14. For a creative attempt to reinstate the (natural) sciences, and its critique, as part of the ongoing religious history of the West, cf. B. Szerszynski, 2005, *Nature, Technology and Sacred*, Oxford: Blackwell.

Contributors

MARCELLA ALTHAUS-REID is an Argentinian theologian and a Reader in Christian Ethics and Theology in the School of Divinity, the University of Edinburgh, Scotland. Her many publications include *Indecent Theology: Theological Perversions in Sex, Gender and Politics* (2001); *The Queer God* (2003); *From Feminist Theology to Indecent Theology* (2005) and *Liberation Theology and Sexuality* (2006).

Address: Faculty of Divinity, New College, University of Edinburgh, Mound Place, Edinburgh, EH1 2LX, Scotland
E-mail: althausm@staffmail.ed.ac.uk

CHRISTOPH BAUMGARTNER, born in 1969, studied Catholic theology and chemistry. From 1998 to 2000 he a held research scholarship of the German Federal Foundation for the Environment (Deutsche Bundesstiftung Umwelt). In 2003, he completed a doctorate in theological ethics with particular consideration of the social sciences at the faculty of Catholic Theology at the University of Tübingen. From 2001 to 2004 he was academic coordinator at the Interdisciplinary Centre for Ethics in the Sciences (IZEW) at the University of Tübingen; since 2004, Lecturer in Ethics in the Faculty of Arts, Department of Theology of the University of Utrecht (Netherlands). His work includes publications on questions of fundamental ethics, on the problem of motivation in ethics (in particular with regard to environmental action) as well as on ethical aspects of bio patenting and nanotechnology.

Address: Utrecht University, Faculty of Theology, Heidelberglaan 2, 3584 CS Utrecht, The Netherlands
E-mail: cbaumgartner@theo.uu.nl

ERIK P. N. M. BORGMAN has been director of the Heyerdaal Instituut of the Radboud University in Nijmegen, an interdisciplinary research institute for theology, science and culture, since 2004. His current research interests are primarily in the area of the cultural and theological significance of contemporary culture. In this area he has published a number of scholarly and popular articles; a collection of essays *Alexamenos aanbidt zijn God* (Zoetermeer, 1994); *Dominicaanse spiritualiteit: Een verkenning*, in Tijdschrift voor Geestelijk Leven (Leuven/Berg en Dal, 2000; ET: *Dominican Spirituality: An Exploration*, London/New York, 2002. Borgman is editorial secretary of the *Tijdschrift voor Theologie* and a director of *Concilium*.

Address: Heyendaal Instituut, Erasmusplein 1, NL-6525 HT Nijmegen, The Netherlands
E-mail: E.Borgman@hin.ru.nl

SHEILA GREEVE DAVANEY is the Harvey H. Potthoff Professor of Christian Theology at Iliff School of Theology, Denver, Colorado. Her most recent books include *Historicism: The Once and Future Challenge for Theology* (Fortress, 2006) and *Pragmatic Historicism: A Theology for the Twenty-First Century* (SUNY, 2000). Her current research is in historicism, pragmatism and liberal theology, especially in American thought, and in the public role of religious discourse and values.

Address: 2201 South University Blvd, Denver, CO 80210-4798, USA
E-mail: sdavaney@iliff.edu

STEPHAN VAN ERP was born in the Netherlands in 1966. He studied theology and philosophy at the Theological Faculty of Tilburg and the Catholic University of Nijmegen, the Netherlands. He taught systematic theology and philosophy of religion at the University of Oxford, UK. He wrote a dissertation on aesthetics and fundamental theology, called *The Art of Theology: Hans Urs von Balthasar's Theological Aesthetics and the Foundations of Faith* (Leuven, 2004). He publishes in the field of systematic and historical theology and philosophy of religion, and is the editor of several books and journals. He is the coordinator of the Department of Theology and Medical Sciences at the Heyendaal Institute of the Radboud University of Nijmegen, the Netherlands. There he works on a project called 'Person, Suffering, Finitude: Towards a Theo-medical Anthropology'. He is also lecturer in systematic theology at the University of Tilburg, the Netherlands. Currently he is a visiting fellow of King's College London, UK.

Address: Heyendaal Institute Nijmegen, Radboud University Nijmegen, P.O. Box 9103, 6500 HD Nijmegen, The Netherlands
E-mail: s.vanerp@hin.ru.nl

Contributors

WILLEM FRIJHOFF was born in 1942. He studied history and social sciences at the Sorbonne and at the École des Hautes Étudees en Sciences Sociales (EHESS) in Paris. From 1971 to 1981 he was research fellow at the EHESS and at the Institut National de Recherche Pédagogique (Paris). From 1983 to 1987 he was Professor for Cultural and Mentality History at the Erasmus University in Rotterdam. He is now Professor for Modern History and Dean of the Faculty of Philosophy at the Free University of Amsterdam. He is a member of the Royal Dutch Academy of Philosophy and the Sciences and President of its Philosophy Section. Publications: numerous articles about different topics of cultural history and history of education (social memory and identity; history of secondary schools and universities; social history of language; cultural transfer and forms of acquisition; popular religion and magic). Current areas of research: mediation of religious experience and models of holiness in early modern Europe and colonial America. Books: (with J. Sperna Weiland), *Erasmus of Rotterdam, the Man and the Scholar* (Leiden, 1988); (with Marijke Gijwijt-Hofstra), *Witchcraft in the Netherlands from the Fourteenth to the Twentieth Century* (Rotterdam 1991); (with Marijke Spies; a synthesis of Dutch culture during the 'Golden Century'), *1650: Bevochten eendracht* (Den Haag, 1999, ET: *1650: Hard-Won Unity* (Assen/Basingstoke, 2004). A collection of his essays on the history of religion: *Embodied belief: Ten Essays on Religious Culture in Dutch History* (Hilversum, 2002).

E-mail: wtm.frijhoff@let.vu.nl

KARL GABRIEL was born in 1943 and studied Catholic theology and sociology in Tübingen (1969) and Bielefeld (1973); he was awarded a PhD in sociology in Bielefeld in 1977 and Habilitation in theology in 1992 in Würzburg. From 1974 to 1980 he was Assistant Lecturer in Bielefeld and from 1980 to 1998 Professor for Sociology, Pastoral Sociology and Caritaswissenschaft at the Katholische Fachhochschule Norddeutschland Osnabrück/Vechta. Since 1998 he has been Professor for Christian Social Sciences at the Katholisch-Theologische Fakultät at the Westfälische Wilhelms-Universität Münster. He is Director of the Institut für Christliche Sozialwissenschaften. Numerous publications in the areas of sociology of religion and the Church, the study of public-sector care organizations and Christian social ethics.

Address: Institut für Christliche Sozialwissenschaften, Hüfferstrasse 27, D-48149 Münster, Germany
E-mail: gabrielk@uni-muenster.de

MARY GREY is currently Professorial Research Fellow, St Mary's University College, Strawberry Hill, London, and formerly D. J. James Profesor of Pastoral Theology at the University of Wales. She was Professor of Feminism and Christendom at the Catholic University of Nijmegen from 1988 to 1992. Recent books include *Sacred Longings: Ecofeminist Theology and Globalisation* (2003), and, with Rabbi Dan Cohn Sherbok, *Pursuing the Dream: A Jewish–Christian Conversation on Reconciliation* (2005). She is a Founder Trustee of the NGO Wells for India, travelling regularly to the semi-desert state of NW India, as well as a trustee of the Dalit Solidarity Network UK, lobbying for the rights of Dalits and other groups suffering caste discrimination.

Address: West Mill, Fullerton Road, Wherwell, Hampshire SP11 7JS, UK

DIEGO IRARRAZABAL was born in Chile in 1942 and is a priest of the Congregation of the Holy Cross. He was director of the Institute of Aymara Studies in Peru from 1981 to 2004 and has been an assessor of church events, workshops and courses in several countries in Latin America. He was President of EATWOT from 2001 to 2006, and since 2005 has worked in a neighbourhood parish and run a formation programme in Chile. His publications include *Religión del pobre y liberación* (1978); *Tradición y porvenir andino* (1992); *Rito y pensar cristiano* (1993); *Cultura y fe latinoamericana* (1994); *Inculturation* (1998, ET 2000); *La fiesta* (1998); *Un cristianismo andino* (1999); *Un Jesús jovial* (2003), *Gozar la espiritualidad* (2004); *Gozar la ética* (2005).

Address: Casilla 238, Correo 11, Santiago, Chile
E-mail diegoira@hotmail.com

PALMYRE M. F. OOMEN is coordinator of the Exact Sciences section at the Heyerdaal Institute of the Radboud University in Nijmegen and Professor of Philosophy at the Technical University of Eindhoven. Thematic focuses of her work are: philosophical-theological understandings of the doctrine of God in relation to humanity and to the world, for the problem of suffering and the autonomy of the world; methodological aspects of theology and natural sciences; particular issues: causality, freedom, teleology, evolution, neurosciences. Publications: *Werkelijkheid: Over materie en geest, alfa en béta, en de Zaak van wiijsbegeerde*, (Inaugural lecture Eindhoven, 2003); together with J. Osse u. V. Kirkels (eds), *Hersenen – Bewustzijn – Zicht op onszelf,* (Nijmegen, 2001); *Doet God ertoe? Een interpretatie van Whitehead als bijdrage aan een theologie von Gods handelen* (Kampen 1998; 2nd rev. edn: 2004).

Address: Heyendaal Instituut, Radboud Universiteit, Erasmusplein 1, NL-6625 HT Nijmegen, The Netherlands
E-mail: p.oomen@hin.ru.nl

RICHARD H. ROBERTS held the Chair of Divinity at the University of St Andrews (1991–95) and then a Chair in Religious Studies at Lancaster University from 1995 until his retirement in 2002. His self-authored and edited publications include *Hope and Its Hieroglyph: A Critical Decipherment of Ernst Bloch's 'Principle of Hope'* (1990); *A Theology on Its Way: Essays on Karl Barth* (1992); *The Recovery of Rhetoric: Persuasive Discourse and Disciplinarity in the Human Sciences* (1993); *Religion and the Transformations of Capitalism: Comparative Responses* (1995); *Nature Religion Today: Paganism in the Modern World* (1998), *Time and Value* (1998) and *Religion, Theology and the Human Sciences* (2001). He is currently working on a *Critique of the Social-Scientific Study of Religion* in which he seeks to interpret the recomposition of the religio-spiritual field in the context of globalization and the modern/postmodern matrix.

Address: Department of Religious Studies, Lancaster University, Lancaster LA1 4YG, UK
Email: r.roberts@lancaster.ac.uk

ELAINE WAINWRIGIT is Professor of Theology and Head of the School of Theology at the University of Auckland, New Zealand, a position she took up in 2003 following twenty years as Lecturer in Biblical Studies in the Brisbane College of Theology and the School of Theology at Griffith University. Her areas of research expertise are gospel studies, especially the Gospel of Matthew, and biblical hermeneutics where her particular interests are in feminist, ecological, postcolonial and contextual perspectives. She heads the Research Unit, Christianity in Aotearoa New Zealand and Oceania, in the School of Theology.

Address: The School of Theology, The University of Auckland, 24 Princes Street, Auckland, New Zealand
E-mail: em.wainwright@auckland.ac.nz

FELIX WILFRED was born in Tamilnadu, India in 1948. He is Professor in the School of Philosophy and Religious Thought, State University of Madras, India. He has taught, as visiting professor, in the universities of Nijmegen, Münster, Frankfurt am Main, and Ateneo de Manila. He was also a member of the International Theological Commission of the Vatican. He has been President of the Indian Theological Association, Secretary of the Theological Commission of FABC. He is a member of the Board of Directors of *Concilium*. His research and field-studies today cut across many disciplines in the humanities and the social sciences. Among his publications in the field of theology: *From the Dusty Soil: Reinterpretation of Christianity* (1995); *Beyond Settled Foundations: The Journey of Indian Theology* (1993); *Sunset in the East? Asian Challenges and Christian Involvement* (1991); *Leave the Temple* (1992).

Address: University of Madras, Dept of Christian Studies, Chepauk, Madras, India
E-mail: fwilfred@satyam.net.in

CONCILIUM

FOUNDERS

A. van den Boogaard
P. Brand
Y. Congar OP †
H. Küng
J.-B. Metz
K. Rahner SJ †
E. Schillebeeckx OP

FOUNDATION

Jan Peters SJ (President)
Paul Vos (Treasurer)
Erik Borgman
Daniel Marguerat
Susan Ross
Felix Wilfred

DIRECTORS

Regina Ammicht-Quinn (Frankfurt, Germany)
Erik Borgman (Nijmegen, The Netherlands)
Christophe Boureux OP (Lyon, France)
Lisa Sowle Cahill (Boston, USA)
Eamonn Conway (Limerick, Ireland)
Hille Haker (Frankfurt, Germany)
Diego Irarrazaval (Santiago, Chile)
Maureen Junker-Kenny (Dublin, Ireland)
Solange Lefevbre (Montreal, Canada)
Daniel Marguerat (Lausanne, Switzerland)
Eloi Messi Metogo (Yaoundé, Cameroun)
Susan Ross (Chicago, USA)
Janet Martin Soskice (Cambridge, UK)
Jon Sobrino SJ (San Salvador, El Salvador)
Luiz Carlos Susin (Porto Alegre, Brazil)
Andrés Torres Queiruga (Santiago de Compostela, Spain)
Marie-Theres Wacker (Münster, Germany)
Elaine Wainwright (Auckland, New Zealand)
Felix Wilfred (Madras, India)

General Secretariat: Erasmusplein 1, 6525 HT Nijmegen, The Netherlands
http://www.concilium.org
Manager: Baroness Christine van Wijnbergen

Concilium Subscription Information

February	2006/1: *The New Pontificate: A Time for Change?*
April	2006/2: *Theology in a World of Specialization*
June	2006/3: *Women's Voices in World Religions*
October	2006/4: *African Christianities*
December	2006/5: *Resurrection*

New subscribers: to receive *Concilium 2006* (five issues) anywhere in the world, please copy this form, complete it in block capitals and send it with your payment to the address below.

Please enter my subscription for *Concilium 2006*

Individuals
____ £35.00 UK/Rest of World
____ $67.00 North America
____ €60.00 Europe

Institutions
____ £48.50 UK/Rest of World
____ $93.50 North America
____ €80.00. Europe

Please add £17.50/$33.50/€30 for airmail delivery

Payment Details:
Payment must accompany all orders and can be made by cheque or credit card
I enclose a cheque for £/$/€ ____ Payable to SCM-Canterbury Press Ltd
Please charge my Visa/MasterCard (Delete as appropriate) for £/$/€ ____
Credit card number ....
Expiry date ....
Signature of cardholder ....
Name on card ....
Telephone .... E-mail ....

Send your order to *Concilium*, SCM-Canterbury Press Ltd
9–17 St Albans Place, London N1 ONX, UK
Tel +44 (0)20 7359 8033 Fax +44 (0)20 7359 0049
E-Mail: office@scm-canterburypress.co.uk

Customer service information:
All orders must be prepaid. Subscriptions are entered on an annual basis (i.e. January to December). No refunds on subscriptions will be made after the first issue of the Journal has been despatched. If you have any queries or require information about other payment methods, please contact our Customer Services department.

www.ingramcontent.com/pod-product-compliance
Lightning Source LLC
Chambersburg PA
CBHW070643300426
44111CB00013B/2230